What they are saying...

"Love or Perish is such an open-hearted, intimate book that I felt I was glimpsing the soul of the author who truly cares about the world. It is filled with a passion for God and strives to live in the Holy Presence. These sentiments form the heart of Harold Kasimow's invitation to love together the world into a new way of being, a way that honors each religion's profound witness to the action of the divine in the world. Drawing on his own experience as a Holocaust survivor, Dr. Kasimow engages the reader in a theology of pathos, exemplified in the life and work of Rabbi Abraham Joshua Heschel. Beginning from the premise of God's ultimate concern for all beings, Love or Perish explores similarities and differences found in the religious claim to ultimacy—Jewish, Buddhist, Christian, Muslim, Hindu, etc.—while steadfastly pursuing a path of contemplative interfaith dialogue with humility, tenderness, and hope. A beautiful book."

Beverly Lanzetta
Author of Emerging Heart: Global Spirituality and the Sacred and
The Monk Within: Embracing a Sacred Way of Life

"In this warm, engaging spiritual testament, Harold Kasimow reflects powerfully on how his early experience of hiding from the Nazis as a child in Lithuania shaped his lifelong mission to promote interreligious understanding and mutual concern. After escaping the Shoah and coming to the United States, he met Abraham Joshua Heschel, who became his mentor and model for interreligious engagement. This work is both a loving homage to Heschel and a testimony to a long history of encounters with Christians, Muslims, Hindus, and Buddhists. By interweaving his personal experiences with his academic study of religious traditions, Kasimow presents a powerful narrative of how one person's journey from a nightmare of cruel suffering can motivate interreligious encounters and inspire hope. Highly recommended for all religious and spiritual seekers!"

Leo D. Lefebure
Georgetown University

"Harold Kasimow is a child of the Shoah who has seen his share of horrors and has chosen to use his experiences to make the world kinder. Anyone lucky enough to meet him is immediately taken by the delicate light that shines through his eyes. This light produces spiritual and intellectual enlightenment; it guides you through the most complex issues of faith. And not just your own: through his life and studies, Dr. Kasimow shows that the strength of one's convictions is not a hindrance but can actually serve as a foundation for respectful and loving interfaith dialogue and, ultimately, for a better understanding of others' beliefs and traditions.

An accomplished scholar, Harold rarely attributes anything to himself, instead using every opportunity to promote others, like his prophetic teacher Abraham Joshua Heschel. As this book brilliantly shows, Kasimow champions the miracle of the world's diversity and plenitude, and, like any great teacher, he does it in the most gentle way. He often starts his conversations with "I just want you to know …" In turn, I just want you to know that a world with Harold Kasimow is a wiser and, more importantly, a significantly kinder place."

Leonya Ivanov
Russian writer working on a book about Christian anarchism and social control

" Harold Kasimow has been an inspiring participant and leader in interfaith dialogue for nearly half a century, and the sources and substance of his inspiration are beautifully conveyed throughout this book. The fruit of immense learning and deep spiritual sensitivity, *Love or Perish*, reveals ways in which the understanding and practice of one's own faith may be enriched through interfaith engagement. This is a book that reflects the openness, warmth, and love that countless students and other dialogue partners have personally experienced in their time with Professor Kasimow."

John Merkle
*College of Saint Benedict
Saint John's University, Minnesota*

"*Love or Perish* is a testimony book. This testimony is exceptionally poignant and reliable. Harold Kasimov's life experience should not lead to optimism. His childhood was marked by the nightmare of the Holocaust, which he miraculously escaped like his master Abraham Joshua Heschel. However, like Heschel, he devoted his entire life to learning and passing on to others the beauty of his own Jewish tradition. However, he did not stop there. The paradoxical tragic beginnings of life taught him to value life itself and those thanks to whom the miracle of life continues.

Love or Perish is a record of transformative meetings with the spiritual masters of our time. Among them, the star of Abraham Joshua Heschel shines brightest. However, Harold did not stop in admiration for his beloved master but treated him as a guide through other religious traditions, especially Buddhism, Hinduism, Islam, and Christianity. Each of them enriched the experience of Judaism by revealing its dimensions and layers that remained hidden for hundreds of years.

I witnessed a series of lectures that Harold gave in May 2004 in Krakow. They were primarily devoted to Judaism and its dialogue with other religions (published in book form *The Search Will Make You Free: A Jewish Dialogue with World Religions* in 2006). It was a novelty for Polish students. Most of them met for the first time with a religious pluralist who not only spoke of the transforming power of interreligious dialogue but was a living example of this transformation. Moreover, he proved that dialogue and respect for other religious traditions is a real alternative to all fundamentalisms. Only a few knew that he was a Holocaust survivor. *Love or Perish* is a record of the victory of the power of spirituality and the light of religion that dispels the darkness of evil and hatred. This reading restores faith in man and his ability to go beyond his own limits."

Stanisław Obirek
American Studies Center, University of Warsaw

"In this book, Kasimow embodies the kind of interfaith dialogue that he has learned as a Holocaust survivor and student of Abraham Heschel: to approach other religions with an openness to their truth that is as deep as the commitment one has to one's own. Written with clarity and conviction, Kasimow's "survivor's perspective" is both unique and inspiring."

Paul Knitter
Paul Tillich Emeritus Professor,
Union Theological Seminary, New York

"Harold Kasimow has long been an important voice in the dialogue about dialogue, especially the dialogue about engaged dialogue, the intersection of contemplation and action. This book puts on full display the sources of that distinctive voice. Shaped by the desperate silence of survival and the elected silence of disciplined meditation, the challenges of global displacement, and the blessings of transformative study with the great souls of history's most violent age, Kasimow speaks the language of prophecy we need to hear today. He is one of the world's most articulate apologists for love. This is the book readers of Professor Kasimow have been waiting for."

Peter A. Huff
*Author of "What Are They Saying About Fundamentalisms?"
and "Atheism and Agnosticism: Exploring the Issues"*

"A simple note to readers: Though there are few tears displayed by the author, Dr. Kasimow's insights bring forth tears and understanding from each reader. He writes to bind people together, with high academic insight, tempered by surviving the Holocaust in his youth yet refined by being Heschel's student and disciple.

Exploring two dozen theological approaches in an honest search for commonalities among Catholic, Muslim, Hindu, and Jewish thinkers, Dr. Kasimow brings out with honest and yet academic care how we become sensitive to the sanctity of life and whether we can discern God's involvement in history. Best of all, Prof. Kasimow introduces us to the insights of modern streams of Buddhism with emphasis on the questions of suffering; the roles attributed to God in Western religions; and the means of living with compassion in this world. By offering sources in context and setting them to speak to the same issues, Professor Kasimow avoids a soft popular approach of simply presenting spiritual paths.

Here you will find a thorough, interesting, and compassionate invitation to extend your own religiosity or further your academic perspective. Here you will witness dynamic exchanges between members of differing religious traditions, who are sure of the gifts of their own faith but were not always initially confident of the treasures they would discover in another's. For all students, professors, and religious leaders, Professor Kasimow's guidance is one precious gift."

John S. Schechter
Conservative Emeritus Rabbi and Instructor at the National Jewish Center for Learning and Leadership

"The Love or Perish Table of Contents at first suggests a series of related but rather different essays by various scholars. What the reader discovers, though, is a wonderfully coherent reflection on the interfaith experience, as the subtitle promises, by a survivor of the Holocaust. Harold's profoundly moving recollections of his childhood experiences of life in hiding set the stage for the book's unfolding meditation on the goodness of the world in the face of evil. And his countless encounters with the followers of other religious paths inform the critical questions he poses. The result is splendid. Do interreligious encounters and dialogue hold promise or peril? Are Eastern and Western religions convergent or starkly divergent? Does faithfulness to one's own tradition demand the denial of other ways or encourage openness to them? We meet some sterner, more exclusivist thinkers in Judaism, Christianity, and Islam; but we also encounter the broader inclusivist or pluralist spirit expressed in the voices of Abraham Joshua Heschel, Hans Küng, Paul Knitter, Seyyed Hossein Nasr, the Dalai Lama, and others. Love or Perish is at once an uplifting and a deepening book, a celebration of interreligious engagement and a glimpse of the ways of world-mending. It's a joy."

Jim Kenney
Global Interreligious Movement Veteran, Founding Trustee and Former Global Director of the Parliament of the World's Religions

Love or Perish:

A Holocaust Survivor's Vision for Interfaith Peace

Harold Kasimow

Published by iPub Global Connection, LLC
www.iPubGlobalConnection.com
1050 W. Nido Avenue, Mesa, AZ 85210
info@iPubGlobalConnection.com

All rights reserved. No part of this book may be reproduced in any way without the expressed written permission of the publisher.

Library of Congress Control Number 2021919562

Copyright © October 21, 2021

ISBN Kindle: 978-1-948575-54-6

ISBN Paperback: 978-1-948575-55-3

About iPub Global Connection

You've opened the right book from the iPub international library. You might be a scholar, an avid reader, a mother or father, a teacher, a 'tween or teen, or one of the rest of us.

Welcome home to iPub Global Connection, where knights of old and now digital nomads from all over the world meet safely to share ideas, find resources, and support individuals whose voices wish to be heard to create and protect the world for your great-great-grandchildren.

We are committed to the empowerment of each and all individuals' contributions to a better world. Often, people may feel paralyzed by the limiting doubt that alone we have no ability or opportunity to make any real impact. When that thought comes up, pick up your keyboard in your mind's eye and type "backspace, delete." Individually, together, we can and will influence others, causing important changes to ensure a habitable world for three generations…A world-embracing global citizenship one by one.

How would *you* begin to define global citizenship? One way might be to remain open enough to learn about other cul tures and people so that we can connect with all. There are, of course, many ways—through music, art, blogs, podcasts, philosophy—all of which help children model how to be better citizens.

Here you may find what you're looking for, the idea you'd like to expand ... a place to be open, to learn, and to trust.

Read on and become a part of the ongoing conversations. Email a note, comment, or share your idea or blog post. Don't keep your views or us a secret. Your voice counts, and we care.

This world is in dire need of love, patience, and respect, and iPub Publishing is a place where you may find a sentinel in the direction to achieve this transformation. We, along with you, can be a guide towards world peace, improving communication through dialogue and advancing diplomacy among nations to engage with differences. Our international writers, authors, thinkers, and scholars are here to make you think… **Join the renaissance!**

iPub Global Connection, LLC
www.iPubGlobalConnection.com
1050 W. Nido Ave.
Mesa, AZ 85210
info@iPubGlobalConnection.com

Other iPub Global Connection books can be found at https://www.iPubGlobalConnection.com.

Dedication

This book is dedicated to Leonard Swidler, who inspired me to write this text when I thought there really wasn't another book in me, and to my dear friend, Reverend Alan Race, who has devoted his life's writings to creating an understanding of other religious traditions in order to eradicate senseless hate.

Acknowledgments

First and foremost, I am grateful to Aron Hirt-Manheimer and Susan Nunn, my editors, who devoted many hours to this book. Thank you both for your kindness throughout the editorial process. Aron first formulated more than a dozen questions that helped me to focus on important events in my life for me to write the introduction. Susan deserves credit for turning it into the final book.

This volume was originally suggested to me by Professor Leonard Swidler. His invitation was the spark for this book. To Leonard and to our mutual friend, Alan Race, who wrote the foreword, I am pleased to dedicate this book. May this book be worthy of its dedication to them. I am also grateful to the editorial staff of iPub Global Connection, especially Sandy Mayer and Sandi Billingslea, for providing a guiding hand to the entire process of publication and for helping me shape the final draft.

I am particularly honored that Peter A. Huff, Leonya Ivanov, Paul Knitter, Jim Kenney, Beverly Lanzetta, Leo D. Lefebure, John Merkle, John S. Schechter, and Stanislaw Obirek found time to consider this book so thoughtfully.

I am grateful to my students at Grinnell College, especially those who have continued to stay in touch with me decades after they graduated. They remind me of the words of Rabbi Hanina, "I have learned much from my teachers, more from my colleagues, but most from my students." I am especially grateful to the following: Barbara

Von Schlegell '75, Michael Chessler '76, Robert Gehorsam '76, Jonathan Herman '77, Amanda Amend, '78, Nathaniel Borenstein '80, John Schechter '79, Lynn Flickinger '83, Henry Rietz '89, Tara Jernigan '95, Jeetander Dulani '98, Melanie Keenan LeGeros '98, Moses Mason '99, Jonathan Rathsam '03, and Katie Kiskaddon '05. I am quite certain this list is not complete.

I am thankful to all my friends and colleagues at Grinnell College, especially to the Religious Studies Department, the German Department, and Dan and Jan Gross from the French Department. Their constant support was very precious to me.

I also want to express my profound gratitude to my dear friend Angela Winburn with whom I have worked for over 20 years. She is a great joy to work with, and I am deeply thankful to her for her devoted efforts, her patience, and good humor.

I am also indebted to Russell Tabbert for reading and providing feedback on several chapters in this book when they were first written.

As always, I want to thank my family. Living with a survivor of the Shoah presents unique problems, and I am forever grateful for their love and understanding. Ultimately, this book is a token of my deep appreciation for my loving mother and my father, an ordinary person who became extraordinary during the Holocaust, who risked his life every day during the war to save his family from the Nazis. He is one of the many unknown heroes of the Holocaust.

Table of Contents

Foreword 1

Introduction 5

Chapter 1 Wrestling with God: Jewish Theological Responses to the Holocaust 35

    Richard Rubenstein 39

    Emil Fackenheim 40

    Abraham Joshua Heschel: Living with the Holocaust 43

Chapter 2 Paths to Jewish Holiness 51

    Moses Hayyim Luzzatto 56

    Rabbi Israel Salanter and the Musar Movement 63

    Abraham Joshua Heschel: A Jewish Saint of the Twentieth Century 64

Chapter 3 Heschel's View of Religious Diversity 69

    The Exclusivist View 71

    The Inclusivist View 72

    The Pluralist View 72

Chapter 4 "To Be is to Stand For" 79

Chapter 5 Swami Vivekananda and Rabbi Abraham Joshua Heschel: Saving the World 91

Chapter 6 Pope John Paul II: A Jewish Perspective on a Polish Catholic Saint 99

Chapter 7 Three Modern Muslim Perceptions of Judaism and Christianity 109

Sayyid Abul A'la Mawdudi 110

Isma'il Raji al Faruqi 111

Seyyed Hossein Nasr 113

Chapter 8 Reflections on Jewish and Christian Encounters with Buddhism 117

The Jewish-Buddhist Encounter 118

The Christian-Buddhist Encounter 121

Three Paths of the Encounter with Buddhism .. 123

Chapter 9 Jewish and Buddhist Responses to Violence 127

Chapter 10 The Lotus Sutra: A Buddhist Path to Mending the World 135

Pope John Paul II on the Buddhist Tradition .. 136

The Lotus Sutra: A Path to Individual and Social Healing and Transformation 139

Chapter 11 A Plea for Religious Humility and Justice 145

Appendix I Photographs 149

Notes 163

Foreword

It is no accident that Harold Kasimow brings his book to a challenging crescendo with the following sentence:

> In closing, may I suggest that in this turbulent time, we all ponder these words of Rabbi Heschel: "We must believe that, morally speaking, there is no limit to the concern one must feel for the suffering of human beings, that indifference to evil is worse than evil itself, that in a free society some are guilty, but all are responsible."

In the face of human suffering, to make a bid for academic neutrality in ethical and religious discourse represents an abdication of moral responsibility. If there is a single thread of purpose, whether implicit or explicit, woven through all of Harold's scholarly writings in religious studies, it can be located here. Learning from his beloved mentor, teacher, and inspirer, Abraham Joshua Heschel, Harold knows that any pretense to neutrality is a veil that needs tearing down.

There are experiences and reasons informing Harold's plea that responsibility takes center stage in religious reflection on human relationships, and especially so "in this turbulent time." They can be identified in a remarkable contribution to the *A BOOK by ME* series, a publishing project which provides a vehicle for young people (you must be under 18 years of age to qualify) to discover a talent for telling stories of genuine inspiration, mainly of holocaust experiences but including other disturbing human rights abuses, to preserve them for future generations. Titled tellingly enough, *The Boy in the Grave,* 12-year-old Chaz Walk relates how Harold, at aged four years, hid from Nazi persecution with his parents and two sisters, first in an attic, then in a forest, and finally in total darkness underground below a cow shed for 19 months and five days. Following the ending of the Second World War, the family made their way to the United States, and Harold eventually pursued a career as a university teacher in religious studies, rising to the ranks of professor in a significant liberal arts university. This journey from child-survivor to university professor is remarkable by any stretch of the imagination.

It was in later years that Harold began to involve himself more deeply and personally in Holocaust history and theology. His motivation was partly to understand himself more thoroughly and partly to educate others so that the memory of the terror is not lost. A central aspect of the meaning of responsibility in the face of indifference to evil is the command to remember, and therefore to educate, so that evil should never be repeated. Moral responsibility, remembering, and education are central values for Judaism and represent a good portion of the Jewish gift to the world. In this sense, Harold stands in a long line of Jewish scholars who have toiled to keep these gifts alive for the sake of deepening our human hold on goodness and truth.

For Harold that hold on goodness and truth is intimately connected with the rise of the significance of interreligious dialogue and comparative studies. If there is a dominant motif within the chapters of this book, it is this. Given his personal history and admiration for Heschel, this is hardly surprising. Again, dialogue for Harold is never a disinterested exercise: it exists as an intrinsic imperative in the search for the truth about the human condition and the pull of self-transcendence. Given Heschel's much-celebrated aphorism that "No man is an island," Harold pursues this truth as both a personal intuition and an academic vocation. This book demonstrates Harold in pursuit of both through dialogues with Buddhist, Christian, Hindu, and Muslim partners, and traditions. He does not glide over substantial differences between traditions, nor does he leave them isolated as islands of self-sufficiency floating in an ocean of postmodern incommensurability. Dialogue represents a binding tie, drawing the religious other into one's own orbit (in Harold's case, the Jewish), yet without absorption or domination. Dialogue is what transpires in the space between our similarities and our differences. Humility in truth-telling is our guiding principle: it's what keeps us human and saves us from idolatry. In this book, humility is not far from the surface of the religious understanding it seeks.

The Judaism of Abraham Joshua Heschel hovers over many of the chapters in this book, directly or indirectly. The master and disciple share a Polish background, and both are fellow Holocaust survivors. In his theology, Heschel inverted the modernist preoccupation with its agonizing human search for God in a seemingly godless world and talked instead of God's search for human beings. This led him to affirm the concept of the pathos of God and its attendant puzzle over what meaning, if any, can be ascribed to the omnipotence of God, given both the reality of human suffering and the givenness of human freedom. Heschel was clear about the pathos but remained unresolved about the omnipotence. Harold shares in these theological conundrums, especially in pondering the presence/absence of God during the Holocaust. But, unlike Heschel, Harold stretches the theological canvass by setting these conundrums alongside, for example, the Buddhist notion of the *bodhisattva*, whose purpose as "magnificent messiahs" renders them agents of society's justice as well as routes to personal transformation. The possibilities for learning across many seemingly religious dissonances are potentially myriad.

I first met Harold Kasimow on a grassy knoll at the Parliament of the World's Religion meeting at Cape Town, South Africa, in December 1999. At the conference, we marched behind the international AIDS quilt in solidarity with scapegoated victims, engaged with religion and spirituality concerning the critical issues of the world, listened to the inspirational Nelson Mandela, but mostly enjoyed one another's company as we exchanged ideas on dialogue, identity, tradition, and pluralism. Although we had known about each other's work prior to our encounter in person, it was a pleasure to experience the harmony between the person and theological work. Since then, we have continued to share insights and learn from one another in true friendship and dialogical spirit.

In this book, Harold insists on the value of interreligious dialogue for the sake of the world's peace, justice, and sustainability. His voice is never angry, but neither does it shy away from calling us to the human vocation to practice compassion with all our might. As Heschel reminds us, "All are responsible."

Alan Race
Anglican Priest, Theologian,
Chair of the World Congress of Faiths,
Editor of the international journal Interreligious
Insight, and author of numerous works in the
theology of interreligious dialogue and relations

Introduction

This book has been on my heart for a long time. For an even longer time, I refrained from even speaking of the Holocaust, as I thought it best discussed by those who were adults at the time that it happened, and I was just a child then. But there comes a time to tell a story. This is the time. This book emerges now because it is time to tell this story, my story, and speak of a solution to a serious problem. It is a solution as to how all of us can live together in peace. This book explores the imperative of humility, ongoing interpersonal dialogue, and the need for inclusion in all things.

This book speaks broadly to the why of an epic tragedy like no other in our history, the Holocaust. Each chapter addresses specific questions around this issue and attempts to present proposed solutions to the inevitable issues: how the Holocaust could happen, the search for meaning and blame, how could God allow this to happen, and the struggle to rise above it after all the suffering. The horror was and is real. The indifference to human suffering was and remains rampant. How does a person or a society learn from such a horrific example of human depravity and indifference? Mass murder and suffering on an unimaginable scale open wounds that may never completely heal. In fact, during this time, the very soul of humanity was laid bare, and we had to find a path back from the brink of its total loss... All of us.

My own thoughts and perspectives are blended here in this narrative with the insight of select scholars and thinkers, some personal associates, and mentors, each addressing aspects of this tragedy. All of us not only address the realities of the Holocaust but humanity's collective future and collective responsibility to each other.

So, where do we go from here? We are standing at a very real crossroads, you and I, with a cosmic choice: learn to live and love together or perish together. It is that simple. Clearly, we have the capacity to do horrible things to each other, sometimes in the name of nationalism, sometimes in the name of a conjured and vengeful, bloodthirsty god. Sometimes, just because we can. Sometimes, just from evil itself. But we also can love and respect each other and help each other achieve greatness.

There is a simple choice. Just because we are capable of monstrous evil, should we then just be evil or indifferent to it? Or should we rise above it? Life has always been about choices, our choices, of what to do or what to become. It has always been about our belief in ourselves, our God, our fellows, and our future together. The choice of which path to follow is ours to make.

We must choose to include all of us in our collective future. We must choose to always be aware of human suffering wherever and whenever we find it and take significant and immediate steps to stop suffering by our collective concern for each other.

This book follows a simple outline in addressing the previously unthinkable. Each chapter tackles a key point in trying to understand what can be incomprehensible and reach a place where moving positively forward is not only possible but absolutely essential. We must embrace our commonality, our collective humanity and secure a future through meaningful interpersonal dialogue and mutual respect. The chapters:

- Chapter 1, titled "Wrestling with God: Jewish Theological Responses to the Holocaust," features contributions and thoughts from Richard Rubenstein, Emil Fackenheim, and my mentor, Rabbi Abraham Joshua Heschel. Each of these men speaks to a central question of "Where was God?" during the Holocaust. It is a fundamental question of meaning and doubt that touches the core of Judaism.
- Chapter 2, Titled "Paths to Jewish Holiness," addresses how to live an enlightened and holy life as a Jew. Perspectives are offered from Moses Hayyim Luzzatto, Rabbi Israel Salanter and the Musar Movement, and Abraham Heschel.
- Chapter 3 summarizes the life and significant contributions of Rabbi Heschel, who concludes that living a good life is "a work of art." It is an ongoing work in progress for all of us... respect for diversity and getting along figure prominently in the discussion of how to love together.
- Chapter 4, "To Be is to Stand For," examines morality and responsibility as crucial to the core of an observant life. Modern life is not a spectator sport as it often requires standing firmly for righteousness and helping others. Doing nothing or being indifferent to suffering is not an option.
- Chapter 5, "Saving the World," addresses the thoughts of Swami Vivekananda and Abraham Joshua Heschel around the importance of meaningful dialogue between and among all religions as a bridge toward better understanding between various people.

- *Chapter 6, "Pope John Paul II: A Jewish Perspective on a Polish Catholic Saint," illustrates the significant contribution of this catholic pope toward healing the rift between Judaism and Catholicism.*
- *Chapter 7, "Three Modern Muslim Perceptions of Judaism and Christianity," explores different Muslim perspectives on God, man, and other religions.*
- *Chapter 8, "Reflections on Jewish and Christian Encounters with Buddhism," looks at Jewish encounters with Buddhism in the search for meaning and connection.*
- *Chapter 9, "Jewish and Buddhist Responses to Violence," focuses on similarities uncovered by both religions in explaining and living with human violence.*
- *Chapter 10, "The Lotus Sutra: A Buddhist Path to Mending the World," discusses the Buddhist journey to personal healing and fulfillment.*
- *Chapter 11, "A Plea for Religious Humility and Justice," summarizes the absolute importance of standing for what is right and just and of not being indifferent to the pain and suffering of other human beings.*

Some Background

It was the resurgence of antisemitism and Holocaust denial that convinced me of the need to share my story in these more recent years. Talking about that period or the passage of time has not eased the trauma.

People ask, "What was it like? How did it affect your life as a child survivor?"

My memories of the Holocaust never really go away. I live with immense anxiety. We survivors all have scars from wounds that we will carry always. I live every day of my life with the painful knowledge that of the one million Jewish children in Poland in 1939, I am one of only about 5,000 who survived. Outside of my immediate family, nearly all my relatives were murdered in the Holocaust.

My children have been affected as well, though I rarely spoke to them about the Holocaust. I now have more frequent dreams related to those years, including a recent dream of being in the *grub* (Yiddish for grave).

I am very loyal and loving to my family and friends, but even now, after all these years, it still takes me a long time to put my trust in strangers. Whenever I have traveled to Europe for a conference or lecture tour and met people who are older than me, especially in Germany, Poland, and Lithuania, I couldn't help but wonder what they did during the war, although I never asked. Being a peaceful person, I have no tolerance for hate and imagine myself being capable of violence if confronted by a mass murderer like Heinrich Himmler or Heydrich Reinhard.

On the other hand, I am deeply moved whenever witnessing an act of kindness or reading about people who have risked their own lives to save others. I remain very grateful to the priest in Dryswiaty who warned my father to run for his life and to the farmer, Vladiaslav Kazimierovich Pivorovich, who let us hide under his barn for nineteen months and five days.

It all began for us on July 2, 1941, just before my fourth birthday, when the German army occupied our village of Dryswiaty, near Vilnius, Lithuania. We were one of the five families who were left in Dryswiaty to work for the Germans. My father had a successful fishing business that employed as many as 60 people, most of whom were non-Jews, and the Germans needed fish.

But, on April 3, 1942, we decided to flee after a priest informed my father that many Jews in the nearby village of Braslov had been massacred. By then, most of the Jews in the area had already been murdered. I know that on August 26, 1941, 2,569 Jews from our area, including all the Jews from Turmont and Dryswiaty, were taken to the Krakyne Forest near Duguciai village and murdered by Germans and members of the Lithuanian Activist Front.

With the aid of several Christian farmers who were willing to risk their lives to save my parents, my two older sisters, and me, we found hiding spots in barns, attics, and other places... Moving from place to place subjected us to many dangers. We once found ourselves on a little boat in the middle of a river when Russian and German troops opened fire on each other from opposite shores. I nearly drowned before we somehow managed to get to the Russian side.

After we all became sick with terrible coughs, people no longer allowed us near their homes. So, my father dug a deep ditch in the forest where we hid for five weeks.

Our next hideout was a bunker my father dug underneath the barn of a farmer he knew. We holed up in that dark, vermin-infested bunker, which we called the *grub* and *kever* ("grave"). With no means to wash, our bodies were crawling with lice.

On the day we left the *grub*, we were huddling beneath a tree in the forest when the shooting broke out all around us. My father went ahead to scout out the situation. We heard a terrible noise and moved away from the tree to see if my father had been hit. A moment later, a rocket struck and destroyed the tree where we had just been sitting. My father returned and told us that a rocket had blown up a horse. Later my parents told me that I had said, *"Ich vill nit shtarbin"* ("I don't want to die.")

We were liberated by the Russian Army in late July 1944 and went back to Turmantas, then under Russian control. We remained there for more than one year before leaving for Lodz, a major center in Poland for Holocaust survivors after the war. During my time in Turmantas, I recovered very slowly, often fainting, and on occasion, losing my voice. I don't remember very much about my time there, but what stands out for me is when my mother's first cousin, Shmerke Kaczerginski, the well-known writer and poet, author of *The Destruction of Vilna* (1947), came to see us in Turmantas. I remember how thrilled he was to meet me because seeing a small Jewish child seemed like a miracle to him.

On our train trip from Turmantas to Lodz, our car was separated and left alone on the track. A gang of Polish men tried to break in. My father, with an iron rod in his hands, was ready to defend us. The standoff ended when Polish police arrived and said, "Break it up, boys."

After a short stay in Lodz, a Jewish organization helped us cross the border into Czechoslovakia. I have memories of our night journey on foot over the border into Germany, where we stayed for a short time in a Displaced Persons (DP) camp in Ulm. Due to our poor health (especially of my sister, Miriam), they sent us to the large DP camp in the spa town of Bad Reichenhall, where we could receive better healthcare. We remained there for approximately three years before emigrating to New York on August 23, 1949.

The trip lasted about two weeks. It was a very rough crossing on the, *General Muir,* an American army ship. Everyone in my family but me became ill. My mother was especially ill because she was pregnant with my sister

Minnie. I was the only one in my family who went to breakfast, this being where I had my first orange.

While giving talks, many of you have asked what I attributed our survival to. Luck had a lot to do with it, I am sure, but when we were in the grub, only my father would leave during dark nights to search for food. I believe that some of his former workers gave him what little food they could, even at the risk of their lives. Even those who had very negative images of Jews made an exception for him because he always treated people with dignity and respect. If a German patrol had caught him while he was at a farmer's house, the farmer and his family would have been killed on the spot. So, yes, the courage of the "righteous gentiles" played a major role in our survival.

Several incidents occurred during our years of hiding when I sometimes wondered whether God intervened to save us, but as I look back, I have serious doubts whether divine providence played a role. I agree with Mordecai Kaplan (1881-1983), the founder of Reconstructionist Judaism, born only fifty miles from my birthplace Turmantas, who said, "Not a single one of the numerous theodicies, or attempts of thinkers to reconcile the goodness of God with the existence of evil, has ever proved convincing."

Mostly, I attribute the fact that we were the only Jewish family to have survived from our area to the courage and bravery of my 39-year-old father. He had lived an ordinary life before the war, but during the Holocaust, he became an extraordinary person, a real hero. He not only saved his own family but another Jewish family as well by bringing them with us when we first escaped from Dryswiaty. His perseverance and resilience gave him the strength to never surrender under any circumstances. The fact that he was very powerful—both physically and mentally—was, of course, an enormous help. Looking back, he reminds me of Winston Churchill, who said, "Never give in, never, never, never."

I remember my father had promised to give two houses to the farmer who sheltered us, but this never became a reality. Some have asked if 'that promise' was why Mr. Piworowitz sheltered us and if that made him any less of a hero. To my knowledge, my father did not have a close relationship with Mr. Piworowitz.

For me, a hero is a person whose noble deeds are done without self-interest, but in the case of Mr. Piworowitz, I think he deserved the distinction of righteous gentile by Yad Vashem because he risked his life and the lives of his family to rescue us. Researchers in Belarus informed me recently that Mr. Piworowitz never actually took possession of the two houses promised to him by my father and that he was exiled by the Soviets to Siberia after the war. I will remain forever grateful to this man who saved my family.

Coming to America was a new experience for us all. One of the first things I remember about emigrating is that my parents took me to see a doctor because I was weak, and my hands were shaking. He told them, correctly, that it would take about three years for me to regain my strength. By the age of fifteen, I became quite strong, but my hands never completely stopped shaking.

My first school was the Salanter Yeshiva, where I learned how to speak English with a good Bronx accent. Rabbi Dubin devoted a great deal of time teaching me Hebrew and preparing me for my bar mitzvah. What I enjoyed the most during my first year in the U.S. was being a member of the Samuel Sterner Choir, which gave me the opportunity to sing at weddings every week and to go to the most famous hotels in the Catskill Mountains and Atlantic City for the Jewish holidays. We sang with some of the most famous cantors of the time, including Moshe Koussevitzky and Richard Tucker, with whom I sang at Madison Square Garden.

I next attended Yeshiva University High School, where for the first two years, I was on the rabbinic track and my Jewish studies concentrated on the study of the Talmud. Although I enjoyed studying with the eminent Rabbi Moshe Tendler, I realized that my views were not totally consistent with those of Orthodox Judaism. I switched to the teacher's institute department and devoted much of the next two years of study to Jewish history.

At the age of 19, I enrolled at the Jewish Theological Seminary, where it was my great fortune to have Rabbi Abraham Heschel as my faculty advisor. I took two of his courses. The first was on the philosophy of religion, and the primary text was his book, *"God in Search of Man."* The second was on *"Chumash"* (Bible) and Rashi. Heschel was not happy that the rabbinical students in our class were not already well versed in Rashi's Torah commentaries, so he went very slowly. For homework, he would assign a section of Genesis, and I would stay up all night studying Rashi's interpretation. I distinctly remember the day Heschel called on me in class, and I was fully prepared to answer his question. I danced all the way home from 121st to 161st Street. Heschel would later write a recommendation in support of my application to the Department of Religion at Temple University in Philadelphia.

At the time, I thought that my special relationship with Heschel was due to our both being Yiddish-speaking Holocaust survivors from Poland. I now think it was because he was a real *mensch*, the Yiddish word signifying a person who combines compassion with a passion for truth.

I decided to write my thesis on Heschel and traveled to New York to audit one of his classes. We would meet afterward in his office to discuss topics. After reading my thesis proposal, he wrote some favorable comments to my advisors at Temple University. His encouragement gave me the confidence and strength to move forward. I received my M.A. in Religion in 1971 and my Ph.D. five years later, both from Temple University.

The last time I spoke to Heschel was on Friday, June 30, 1972. He had called me to give me his address in Los Angeles, California, where he was going for the rest of the summer. I was pleasantly surprised by the call; I imagine that he called so that I could reach him if I needed help. Heschel, who devoted his life to love and peace, was for me not just a superlative teacher but my hero. He remains the most important spiritual teacher of my life.

I thought of Heschel as a Jewish saint and still consider him to be so. In *The Earth is the Lord's*, Heschel's beautiful memoir of Eastern European Judaism, he defines the saint as one "who did not know how it is possible not to love, not to help, not to be sensitive to the anxiety of others." In my studies of the world's major religions, I have been particularly attracted to saints, spiritual men and women of great compassion who are not preoccupied with themselves but with the suffering of other people and who never adjust to violence; they dedicate their lives to bringing compassion to the people of our planet. I believe that Abraham Joshua Heschel belongs in this pantheon. In one of his interviews, Heschel said, "I am the most maladjusted person in the world because I can never adjust to violence."

A half-century after his death, Rabbi Heschel is still remembered by many as the greatest Jewish spiritual teacher and activist of his generation. As early as the 1950s and 1960s, some of his students came to see him as a saint of our generation. His teaching of Judaism, which incorporated the insights of both the ethical and mystical streams of Jewish tradition, stirred the hearts and minds of Jews and Christians alike.

Rabbi Heschel devoted his life to teaching, first in Germany until his deportation by the Nazis in 1938, and then at the Hebrew Union College and the Jewish Theological Seminary in New York. I consider Heschel, a great model for our time and an inspiration for the future through learning and social action. In his ground-breaking lecture, "No Religion is an Island," Heschel defines himself as a survivor: "I am a brand plucked from the fire of an altar [to] Satan on which millions of lives were exterminated to evil's greater glory..." I have devoted much time to understanding his radical stress that diversity of religions is the will of God and the need for interfaith dialogue (our traditions are different, our tears are the same.) People of many religious traditions have embraced him as a spiritual guide.

As the most prominent Jewish voice of his time for nonviolent social action, interfaith dialogue, and peace, Heschel had a special friendship with Martin Luther King Jr., with whom he marched from Selma to Montgomery. King called Heschel, "A truly great prophet... Relevant at all times, always standing with prophetic insight to guide us through these difficult days." Several Christian scholars, including the Polish philosopher and theologian Stanislaw Obirek, regard him as a prophet, while some Jews see him as a saint.

For Heschel, "Learning is a religious act," to study is to be in paradise, and to march for justice is like feeling one's "legs praying." His passion for knowledge, truth, and action is especially significant in this critical time, as we struggle through political, social, health, and ecological upheavals. He devoted his life to education, social justice, interfaith dialogue, and the infinite value of every human being. His name is a reminder that we must be scholars and activists for the future and that religious and racial bigotry will always require our collective effort to combat it.

Bernard Phillips, the visionary and founding chair of the religion department at Temple University, was my mentor and role model. I have been living with his spirit all of my academic life. When I met him in 1967, he told me that he was more interested in finding truthful people than in finding the truth and that the sun shines from the faces of truthful people. Whenever I was with him, I felt that the sun was shining.

It was through Phillips that I became fascinated by Asian religions. He introduced me to Hinduism, Buddhism, Chinese thought, and Sufism, the mystical dimension of Islam. I can still remember how moved I was while reading some of the great Hindu scholars, including Sarvepalli Radhakrishnan, Ananda Coomaraswamy, and especially Swami Vivekananda.

Everything I studied with Phillips was new to me, and yet it all aligned with what I had learned from Heschel, who said, "Holiness is not the monopoly of any particular religious tradition... The Jews do not maintain that the way of the Torah is the only way of serving God." According to Heschel, religion is a means, not an end. The aim of religion is to transform us, to have concern for others, which makes us truly human. What was most critical for Heschel, as for Phillips, is not what religion a person belongs to but how human he or she really is, not what tradition a person follows but how he or she lives life.

For Phillips, the truly religious person is the lover of life, and to love life means to be in creative union with life: "Love is the perception of the infinite in the finite."

I am deeply grateful to Dr. Phillips, who has played a major role in how I teach comparative religion and in my becoming active in the dialogue with members of other religious traditions. I also realize that several crucial touchstones of reality for Phillips have become touchstones for me. I try always to remember his caution: "The danger in reading too much about the spiritual, and the danger in attending too many conferences on the spiritual life, is that one may come to imagine that hearing about the truth, talking about the truth, thinking about the truth, reading about the truth is the same thing as the living of the truth."

Another of my great teachers of comparative religion was Wilfred Cantwell Smith (1916- 2000). I had the privilege of studying with him in a National Endowment Summer Seminar titled "Scripture as Form and Concept," which he directed at Harvard University in 1982. Smith, a Presbyterian minister, was very influential in the development of religious studies and Islamic studies in the twentieth century. Many scholars of religion claim that he opened their eyes to their prejudices toward religions other than their own. I still remember how touched he was when I brought him some cookies for his birthday. When I left him a copy of my first article on interreligious dialogue, he called me at home that very evening to express his appreciation. By the end of the seminar, I regarded Smith not only as an original thinker and master teacher but as one of the most gentle, pious people I had ever encountered.

He helped me to understand that the op-ed question I once posed, "Is religion a force for evil or good?"...might not be the most helpful question. Whether religion makes us better or worse, he insisted, depends more on how we *interpret* our sacred texts than on the literal meaning of those texts. Smith would agree with Heschel, who said, "The cardinal sin in thinking about ultimate issues is literal-mindedness." For Smith, religions are not fixed, static entities, and the meanings of sacred texts are in the minds and hearts of the believer. He insisted that they should not be interpreted literally to justify inhumane actions such as slavery and war, but in a manner in which every person is treated as having infinite value. For Smith, holy texts should be in harmony with the universal goodness; that is, they must be consistent with the golden rules found in the ethical teachings of the world's major religions, which share a dream of a world at peace, a world in which each person has immeasurable value. A true encounter with "the other" can give us the capacity to extend love to the stranger and see the divinity of those who profess different belief systems.

If we hope to lessen hate and violence among different religions, their adherents need to focus not only on their own sacred texts but also on the teachings in word and deed of the great spiritual teachers of our era—people like Abraham Joshua Heschel, Thomas Merton, Martin Luther King, the Dalai Lama, St. John XXIII, St. John Paul II, and Pope Francis. What they have in common is a commitment to their own faith while sharing a deep respect for other religious traditions.

When I think of those who continue to press for the supremacy of their own kind at the expense of the other, I remind them what my teacher, Leonard Swidler, Professor of Catholic Thought and Interreligious Dialogue at Temple University and co-founder of the *Journal of Ecumenical Studies* taught me... The future offers two alternatives: death or dialogue. In the words of Rabbi Heschel, "The choice is to love together or to perish together." I live with the Biblical commandment: "Choose life."

Professor Swidler has written more than 80 books, but he is best known for his article, *Dialogue Decalogue: Ground Rules for Interreligious Dialogue,* which has been translated into many languages and is a foundational statement on interfaith dialogue. In this article, Swidler presents "ten commandments" which, he asserts, are essential for genuine interfaith dialogue:

1. The primary purpose of dialogue is to change and grow in the perception and understanding of reality and then to act accordingly.

2. Interreligious dialogue must be a two-sided project—within each religious community and between religious communities.

3. Each participant must come to the dialogue with complete honesty and sincerity.

4. Each participant must assume a similar complete honesty and sincerity in the other partners.

5. Each participant must define himself.

6. Each participant must come to the dialogue with no hard-and-fast assumptions as to where the points of disagreement are.

7. Dialogue can take place only between equals.

8. Dialogue can take place only based on mutual trust.

9. Persons entering interreligious dialogue must be at least minimally self-critical of both themselves and their own religious traditions.

10. Each participant eventually must attempt to experience the partner's religion "from within."

Professor Swidler worked with Hans Küng to draft *A Global Ethic: The Declaration of the Parliament of the World's Religions*, which two hundred religious leaders signed at the 1993 Parliament of the World's Religions. This document aims to lead people of all faiths to recognize the common ethical core in all religious traditions, including humanism, and encourage genuine interfaith dialogue.

Hans Küng is renowned for his insistence that there can be "no peace among the nations without peace among the religions" and "no peace among the religions without dialogue among the religions." What stands out for me in the work of Swidler and Küng is their stress on the equality and dignity of every human being. Swidler's dialogue statement and Küng's global ethic statement are in perfect accord with Heschel's view that "many things on earth are precious, some are holy, humanity is the holy of holies." For Heschel, the fundamental statement about human beings in Jewish tradition is that we are created in the image of God. From this perspective, dialogue aims to develop friendship and love among people. In the Abrahamic faiths (Judaism, Christianity, and Islam), the love of God must manifest itself in love for all human beings.

We read in Leviticus 19:33-34: "Love the stranger as yourself." As Rabbi Jonathan Sacks, of blessed memory, points out, in the Hebrew Bible, "Only one verse commands, 'You shall love your neighbor as yourself,' but in no fewer than in 36 places commands us to 'love the stranger.'" Interfaith dialogue is about making the command to love the stranger a reality and is fully in accord with all the major religious traditions.

I learned a great deal from Professor Swidler about the remarkable similarities of the three Abrahamic faiths. By similarities, I do not mean that they are identical. The differences are real, which is why dialogue is so important, but it is important for us to know what they fundamentally have in common.

All belong to what Pope John Paul II called the "tradition of Abraham." He stated on numerous occasions when speaking to Muslims and Jews: "Your God and ours are one and the same, and we are brothers and sisters in the faith of Abraham."

All believe in the same creator of heaven and earth. Christian Arabs call God "Allah," the same word used for God by Jews and Christians who live in Arabic lands.

All speak of God as holy, just, wise, powerful, loving, compassionate, and all-knowing.

All teach us to love God as a neighbor who communicates with human beings in a caring way. Most important, the Abrahamic traditions stress that every human being is created in the image of God and is precious in God's eyes.

Our duties as human beings are to protest injustice, bring healing, and confront the mystery of evil in the world. No human being can fully comprehend God's ways. The Talmudic sage, Rabbi Yannai, teaches: "We do not know the reason either for the suffering of the righteous or the prosperity of the wicked." We find in the Abrahamic traditions many answers to the problem of evil. Yet, after all, explanations are given, an element of mystery remains because believers will say: Human beings are unable to comprehend the ways of the Almighty fully.

In the foreword to my book, *Interfaith Activism,* Edward Kaplan, my longtime friend, and the author of the definitive biography of Abraham Joshua Heschel, wrote that as a child, I "made a decisive existential step into compassion. The heroism of their decent non-Jewish acquaintances confirmed my belief in the goodness of a great many Polish people and, by extension, of all people." He is essentially correct. Though, I see it more as a continuous process nourished by my parents and yeshiva education, than as a "decisive step." Soon after we arrived in the U.S. in 1949, my parents enrolled me in Yeshiva Salanter in the Bronx. Like other Lithuanian Jews, my parents were familiar with the teachings of Rabbi Israel Salanter, who founded a self-perfection movement in the 1840s known as Musar. In my three years at the yeshiva, I internalized the intention of Rabbi Salanter: to become a *mensch*, a compassionate person who is mindful of relations with others and treats everyone with dignity.

Kaplan is correct in saying that the heroic actions of non-Jews who helped us survive the war contributed to my positive worldview. That is not to say that Jews and Catholics in Poland have always gotten along. It is a complex relationship. During the Nazi occupation, Poles saved us; after the war, Poles nearly killed us. That was long ago. When I returned to Poland for a lecture tour in 2004 after a 60-year absence, my heart was full of gratitude for the record number of courageous Polish people who have been honored by Yad Vashem in Jerusalem as "Righteous of the Nations."

I was deeply moved by the kindness shown to me by the students, professors, and clergy I encountered in Poland. The deep friendships I established with some of them continue to this day, especially with Professor Stanislav Obirek, a former Jesuit and leading intellectual who is a fearless fighter for Jews and Jewish-Christian dialogue. I was especially delighted when he gifted me a hat worn by his mentor, Stanislav Musial, SJ (1938-2004), of blessed memory, a pioneer of Catholic-Jewish dialogue who devoted his life to combating anti-Semitism. Several rabbis from Jerusalem attended his funeral to recite the Kaddish prayer for him, a request he made before he died. In describing Father Musial, his Polish friends often quote Rabbi Abraham Joshua Heschel: "A religious man is a person who holds God and man in one thought at one time, at all times, who suffers harm done to others, whose greatest passion is compassion, whose greatest strength is love and defiance of despair."

Now, I feel a strong sense of urgency to bear witness to my own Holocaust experience and the difficult truth about the murder of six million Jewish people by the Nazis. I hope that telling my own story, combined with the history of the Holocaust, will serve as a warning of how contempt for the other leads to hate, violence, and crimes against humanity. It will also alert people to the danger of silence and indifference and may help to bring greater sympathy for suffering people everywhere in the world.

Since I have devoted my life to the study of different religious traditions, I also have a sense of obligation to educate people about the danger of religious intolerance. There are still too many religious leaders who incite hate among their followers by teaching them that they alone possess the truth and that they are therefore superior to people of other faith traditions. I believe that silence and indifference on the part of religious leaders contributed to the Holocaust.

It took about forty years after my liberation before I began to teach about the Holocaust and another twenty years before I told people about my own experience. Before that time, I felt an obligation to tell my story in the hope that our earth would never again be so "soaked with blood." I felt that it would be better told by people who had witnessed the Holocaust as adults and could remember and make more sense of their experiences than a child survivor, which I alluded to earlier.

I also imagined that no one would believe my story or would want to hear it. When Elie Wiesel first submitted *Night*, one of the most influential Holocaust memoirs, he was told, "Your book is morbid. Nobody wants to hear your stories."

I knew, of course, what had happened to me during and after the war, but I had not read much about the Holocaust before taking up my teaching position in the Religious Studies Department at Grinnell College in 1972. I was not yet aware that during the 1930s, America's leading colleges and universities, including Harvard, Columbia, the University of Wisconsin, and the University of Minnesota, had forged friendly ties with the Nazified universities, inviting top Nazi officials to campus. They also participated in student exchanges with the German universities that expelled all their Jewish faculty members. In May 1933, Germany's student organization began book burnings at their universities, actualizing the prediction of the Jewish-born German poet Heinrich Heine (1797-1856): "When people begin to burn books, burning people may soon follow." I also had no knowledge of the Wannsee Conference, which took place on January 20, 1942, outside of Berlin, where fifteen high-ranking Nazi Party officials formulated what they called the "final solution of the Jewish question." The murder of every Jewish man, woman, and child.

In the 1980s, I finally agreed to teach a course on the Holocaust at Grinnell, although I made no claim to be an expert on the subject. I relied on the teachings and insights of leading historians, theologians, and novelists, such as Yehuda Bauer, Franklin Littell, Primo Levi, and Eli Wiesel. As I began to see more fully the magnitude of this catastrophe, I also realized that the Holocaust defies human comprehension. Finding the subject frightening and depressing, I offered the course only twice. Worst of all, the realization that the genocide was not only carried out by a group of deranged madmen but also by ordinary people. The top Nazi ranks included scholars, artists, jurists, doctors, university professors...including the eminent German philosopher, Martin Heidegger.

The best I could do was to devote about two weeks of my "Introduction to Judaism" course to the Holocaust as part of Jewish and world history that must never be forgotten, denied, or repeated. I always make the point that the six million Jews, including one million children, were not the only victims; at least five million non-Jews, including Roma people, homosexuals, and Jehovah's Witnesses, and as many as three million Polish Catholics, including many priests and nuns, were also exterminated as part of the Nazi campaign to "purify humanity." We also now know that Heinrich Himmler had a plan to eventually exterminate all the Slavic people.

It was not until 2001 that I felt ready to attend a conference of Holocaust survivors which took place in Vilnius, Lithuania; and I did not speak publicly about my experience as a Holocaust survivor until 2004, when my dear friend Brother Wayne Teasdale invited me to address the Parliament of World Religions in Barcelona, Spain. Prior to that event, I had not revealed to my students that I was a Holocaust survivor because I did not feel like a victim and did not want anyone to see me as one.

Dr. Eva Fleischner, an early pioneer of Catholic-Jewish dialogue who devoted her life to teaching about the horrors of the Holocaust, was once asked why she continues to teach such a painful subject. She replied: "No other course forces my students and me to the same extent to confront the depths to which the human spirit can sink and also, here and there, to the heights to which it can rise." Her response resonates with me.

At this point in my life, I have spoken on the Holocaust at schools, synagogues, colleges, and universities in several countries, sharing what I have learned from my family's war experience and the core messages of most survivors I have encountered in my life:

- Do not hate
- Love life
- Welcome the stranger
- Defend people of all faiths
- Never give up hope that peace will come

Speaking of defending people of all faiths, in my early adulthood, I developed a desire to study as many religions as possible. Since then, I have had the great opportunity to pursue that goal, and in the process, I have been spiritually enriched by each of the world's great religions that I have studied. To illustrate how interfaith learning and engagement have enriched my life, here I will focus on my encounter with Buddhism, which first came by reading *Siddhartha* by

Herman Hesse. At the time, I was working at Marboro Bookstore in New York City and studying at the Jewish Theological Seminary. I later reread the book while I was a graduate student at Temple University, and I used it as a text for my "Introduction to Asian Religions" course at Grinnell College.

In this book, Hesse tells the story of a young Hindu Brahmin who lives during the time of the Buddha. Like the Buddha, Siddhartha sets out on a journey in search of an authentic, meaningful life—enlightenment. He encounters many fascinating people, including Kamala, a beautiful courtesan who helps him to become rich and teaches him the pleasures of physical love. He also encounters the Buddha, who tells him that life is full of suffering but that there is a way to free oneself from such a fate. Siddhartha is very taken with the Buddha but does not become a follower, realizing he must find his own path. Ultimately, Siddhartha realizes that the most important thing in the world is love. He tells his best friend that we must "love the world and ourselves and all beings with love, admiration, and respect."

Hesse attributes a key life lesson to the Buddha: "I teach but two things, suffering and the release from suffering." This view contrasts radically with the traditional Jewish view that suffering is inexplicable and can only be overcome in the world to come. I find the idea that we can put an end to suffering and be liberated from mental pain very attractive. Other Buddhist ideas that speak to me are the values of generosity and compassion; freeing oneself from greed, hate, and jealousy; and being open to other religious paths. But the idea that moves me more than any other in most forms of Buddhism is that of the *bodhisattva* – the ideal person – characterized by their great love and compassion for human beings. Robert Thurman, the foremost scholar of Tibetan Buddhism, calls bodhisattvas "Buddhist messiahs."

In aiming to create a world of earthly bliss and moral perfection for all humanity, bodhisattvas do not separate their enlightenment from that of all human beings, who are to be treated as if they were their own mothers. This Buddhist vision to bring about a complete transformation of humanity aligns with the central Jewish idea of *Tikkun Olam* (repairing the world).

I had my second, though limited, encounter with Buddhism when I served in the U.S. Army in Okinawa and Thailand (1961-1963). On several occasions, I visited magnificent temples with amazing Buddhist statues in Bangkok. Several Buddhist monks I had met impressed me with their abundance of friendliness and compassion. These and other experiences in southeast Asia, especially in Thailand, influenced me to take courses in Asian religions when I enrolled at Temple University.

My serious study of Buddhism and Hinduism began while I was a graduate student at Temple University. Richard DeMartino, an assistant to D. T. Suzuki and co-author with Erich Fromm of the 1960s classic *Zen Buddhism and Psychoanalysis*, insisted that "intellectual understanding of Zen doesn't cut any ice."

My teacher and advisor, Bernard Phillips, taught me that to really know a religious tradition, one must personally experience it. Following his guidance, in 1976, I enrolled in a meditation program at the San Francisco Zen Center. A year later, in preparation for teaching a class on the Buddhist tradition, I studied for a summer at the American Institute of Buddhist Studies in Massachusetts with Robert Thurman and several other Buddhist teachers and for the first time practiced Vipassana meditation (insight meditation).

I taught a course on Buddhism and delivered several lectures at Waseda University in Tokyo, Japan, in 1988- 89 and spent much of my free time with Ikuo Azuma Roshi at Soji-Ji, the major temple of Soto Zen. We meditated and discussed the affinity between Zen Buddhism and Hasidism. A key idea in both traditions is to "forget the self" and, by so doing, experience a new spiritual dimension. During that year in Tokyo, I conversed with a number of Buddhist priests and Jesuits from Sophia University, among them the Jesuit Zen master Kakichi Kadowaki, author of the well-known work *Zen and the Bible*. I was also a member of the Jewish community of Japan and delivered several talks at the synagogue at the request of Rabbi Michael Schudrich.

My most serious encounters with Buddhism began during the mid-90s, when I practiced Buddhist meditation for two summers at San-un Zendo in Kamakura, Japan. At the end of each summer, we always did a Sesshin (5-7-day intensive meditation in a Zen monastery). I also took part in a Sesshin with Aiken Roshi, one of the best-known American-Buddhist teachers. Although I did not experience spiritual enlightenment, at the end of that Sesshin, I quit smoking. I believe this saved my life.

My experiences with Buddhist meditation helped me achieve greater mental clarity and, at times, an inexplicable sense of unity with the universe. Buddhist meditation has also helped me develop a greater attachment to the Jewish tradition. After two summers of practicing Zen meditation at Kamakura, I reread Heschel's book, *Man Is Not Alone,* and saw things that had totally eluded me in previous readings.

Since the end of World War II, many American Jews have been attracted to the Buddhist tradition. While Jews make up only two percent of the American population, it is estimated that at least one-third of Western Buddhists in America are Jewish by birth. Many of the leading Buddhist teachers in America come from Jewish families, including Bernard Glassman, Sharon Salzberg, Joseph Goldstein, Jack Kornfield, Norman Fischer, Bhikkhu Bodhi, Natalie Goldberg, Thubten Chodron, Sylvia Boorstein, Allen Ginsberg, and Lama Surya Das, to name just a few. Ginsberg and Surya Das studied with Chogyam Trungpa, one of the most influential Tibetan teachers in America, who had so many Jewish students that he called his school "the *oy vey* school of Buddhism." I've heard that more than one-fourth of professors teaching Buddhism in American colleges and universities were born Jewish.

I think the reason that so many Jews have turned to Asian forms of spirituality in the last fifty years has to do as much with the way the Jewish tradition has been presented to American Jews as to Buddhism's appealing message.

There are many other reasons why so many Jews have turned to Buddhism. But, to my mind, the major reason was the failure of the Jewish community's teachers and leaders to fully present the spiritual dimension of Judaism in the decades following the traumatizing murder of one-third of the world's Jewish population. It is no surprise that Jewish leaders devoted the bulk of their energies to the physical survival of the Jews and to the creation of the state of Israel. At the same time, yeshivas and other Jewish schools of higher learning did not focus sufficiently on *Aggadah*, the spiritual aspect of Judaism, emphasizing instead on the *halakhic* or legal aspect of the tradition. They concentrated on the mind rather than the heart. At the Jewish Theological

Seminary, Rabbi Abraham Heschel realized this problem when he insisted that *halakhah* without *aggadah* is taking the life element out of Judaism, that religion must be concerned with the inner life. It is little wonder then that some of the most spiritual Jews felt that Judaism was not nurturing their souls, that it was not really a serious spiritual path. And thus, they turned to Buddhism.

From Job to the Holocaust, Jews have wrestled with the question of why the innocent suffer. When Rabbi Shlomo Carlebach was asked if he thought the Shoah has been a factor in Jews' being attracted to Buddhism, he answered, "Look—six million corpses can make you mighty angry at God. So, we couldn't learn from our own people. But God is merciful, so he sent us teachers from the Far East, to whom we could listen."

The Buddhist tradition is not concerned with a creator God. Speculation about the existence or nonexistence of God does not lead us to liberation. This may be the greatest distinction between Buddhism and Judaism. The meditation-centered Buddhist groups, which include Theravada Buddhism, Zen Buddhism, and Tibetan Buddhism, all emphasize that only through our own power can we save ourselves. For Western Jewish Buddhists, the Buddha, which means "the awakened one," was just a human being who attained enlightenment without help from any God or supernatural force.

The idea that we have the power to liberate ourselves from pain, grief, and sorrow is central to Buddhist thought. The Buddha said, "I teach but two things—suffering and the release from suffering." But it holds the promise that through the practice of meditation, one will gain insight into one's own mind, which will lead to seeing things clearly and will bring an end to suffering. In one of the most widely used college texts, titled *What the Buddha Taught,* Walpola Rahula claims that the person who attains enlightenment will be "the happiest being in the world... Free from anxiety, serene and peaceful."

One could also argue that it is what Judaism and Buddhism have in common that somehow accounts for Buddhism's magnetism for some Jews. In 1961, U Nu, the prime minister of Burma, and David Ben Gurion, the prime minister of Israel, had a conversation with Edward R. Murrow regarding the similarities and differences between Judaism and Buddhism. Ben Gurion said, "It is similar and different. It is similar in that Buddhism wants people to live in peace, love each other, and help each other, to draw away hatred."

Similarities aside, some Jewish leaders believe that Buddhism and the other Asian religions are forms of idol worship and see exploring other religious traditions, even if undertaken to enrich one's own spiritual path, as being against the will of God. Other Jewish leaders realize that the study of Buddhism and the practice of some forms of Buddhist meditation do not lead to a negation of God but a more spiritual Jewish life. Despite these very different reactions, and there are many more, all Jews believe in the unity of the Jewish people and are sad that so many young Jewish men and women do not find spiritual fulfillment in their own tradition. Jewish leaders would be thrilled to have these young spiritual people who have found a meaningful life in Buddhism return home to Judaism.

Lama Surya Das, who describes himself as a "Jewish boy from Long Island," claims that "Buddhism made me a mensch and brought me happiness" and further states that

Buddhism helped him to "find my place in life and the universe." Like Lama Surya Das, many of the best-known Jewish-born Buddhist teachers in America are helping many Jews deepen their quest for the Jewish tradition. This is especially the case for Zoketsu Norman Fischer, who, together with his friend Rabbi Alan Lew, blessed memory, founded Makor Or, a Jewish meditation center in San Francisco, where they teach Jews Buddhist meditation along with Torah and Jewish prayer.

Rabbi Sheila Peltz Weinberg, another well-known teacher of Buddhism who has remained within the Jewish tradition, says this of her encounter with Buddhism: "The impact of Buddhism on my life as a Jew has been to give me a new lens with which to interpret and understand the sacred teachings of my people and more deeply apply those teachings to my life. To what end? To live with more awareness, more compassion, more wisdom, and more love." To this, I say, Amen

Chapter 1

Wrestling with God: Jewish Theological Responses to the Holocaust

My major focus in this chapter is on influential Jewish theological responses to the Holocaust—in Hebrew, *Shoah*, (catastrophe) and *Hurban* (destruction), written in the 1960s and 1970s by several prominent Jewish rabbis and scholars across denominational lines. Since then, there have been other influential Jewish theological responses, for example, from Hans Jonas in the 1980s and Melissa Raphael in the early 2000s, but in this chapter, I concentrate on major responses from earlier decades.

It should not be surprising that there is a great divide between two camps of early Holocaust respondents. One sees the Holocaust as an unprecedented event, a horror without parallel, and a turning point in history. The other sees it as yet another great tragedy in Jewish history. Both wrestle with the ultimate question: Where was God?

Following World War II, there was little talk of the Holocaust in America, except for a few writers such as Elie Wiesel. It was only in the 1960s and early 1970s that some Jewish and Christian theologians began to seriously struggle with the religious implications of the Holocaust. Among the factors awakening interest were the writings of Elie Wiesel and Primo Levi about their experiences in Auschwitz and the 1963 controversial play *The Deputy* by Rolf Hochhuth, which portrayed Pope Pius XII as having failed to speak out against the Holocaust. Most significantly, there was the trial of the Nazi Adolph Eichmann and the writing of Hannah Arendt on that trial. At the same time, several Holocaust survivors who emigrated to America in the late 1940s and early 1950s began to tell their stories of survival. When they first arrived, they remained mostly silent, realizing that their experiences under the Nazis would be utterly incomprehensible to most Americans. They directed their energy to start a new life for themselves and their children.

I can speak of this from my own experience. I was 11 years old when my family and I arrived in New York in 1949, after spending years in hiding in Poland and, after the war, in a Displaced Persons Camp in Germany. My parents never spoke to my sisters and me about the war, only to other Holocaust survivors. During the years that I was attending Yeshiva University High School and the Jewish Theological Seminary in New York, no one ever spoke about the Holocaust. Even during my graduate school years in religious studies at Temple University in Philadelphia, I never studied the Holocaust.

Confronting the Holocaust means that one must deal with the classic and perennial problem: why is there so much evil and suffering in a world where there is a God of compassion who created human beings in God's own image? How are we to make sense of the world if we have faith in a God of justice and compassion and yet see so much suffering of the innocent?

I turn now to presenting the views of those who see the Holocaust as an unprecedented, unique event, a horror without parallel, a turning point in history, a rupture in Jewish theology that requires a serious rethinking of God's covenant with Israel. The most radical Jewish responses came from Richard Rubenstein, Emil Fackenheim, and the novelist Elie Wiesel. For Wiesel, the Holocaust was "a mutation on a cosmic scale." For Fackenheim, who is seen by many as the most articulate spokesperson of the Holocaust, "the Nazi Holocaust has no precedent in Jewish history." And for Rubenstein, "we live in a time of the death of God." I must point out that Holocaust theologians do not claim that the Holocaust is a "greater or more tragic crime than all others," only that it is unique.

In order to understand how radical these responses were, it is helpful to look at the classical Biblical and rabbinic responses to evil since many Jews, including survivors, have found that traditional Jewish responses still speak to them.

Two central responses to suffering and evil in the world run through the Jewish tradition. The first sees suffering as *mipnei hataeinu*, that is, "because of our sins." The second view is that suffering is a mystery which human beings cannot comprehend. These two responses to suffering are already found in the Book of Job. The idea that suffering is a consequence of sin is the position taken by Job's friends. The basic thesis of Job, however, is that evil is a mystery. We know that God rejected the explanation of Job's friends. But God did not explain to Job why he suffered. Rabbi Yannai, a rabbi in the third century, wrote, "It is beyond our power to understand why the guilty prosper, and the innocent suffer." Rabbi Yannai speaks for a major strand of rabbinic Judaism that teaches that the problem of suffering is incomprehensible from a human perspective.

Although most Holocaust theologians find the idea of divine retribution as a cause of the Holocaust to be obscene, a few prominent modern Jewish thinkers are still perpetuating this view. Rabbi Yoel Teitelbaum (1887–1979), the Rebbe of Satmar, one of the large Hassidic groups from Hungary that later came to New York, "placed the entire blame for the Holocaust squarely upon the shoulders of the Zionist movement. And he insisted that the Messiah will not arrive so long as the State of Israel exists." Rabbi Teitelbaum claimed that the Jews were punished by God because the Zionists took power into their own hands to create the state of Israel without waiting for the Messiah. For him, this goes against the Torah teaching that Jews are in exile by divine decree. According to Rabbi Jonathan Sacks, the former chief rabbi of Britain, although the Satmar Rebbe was an extremist, he was also a "scholar and intellect of great distinction."

On the other hand, Rabbi Menachem Immanuel Hartom (1916-1992), an Israeli Orthodox Rabbi, blames the Holocaust on Jews who wanted to make the diaspora their permanent home; thus, the Holocaust was God's punishment for their anti-Zionism. A most painful response is given by Avigdor Miller (1908–2001), a prominent American Orthodox rabbi, who claims that "Hitler was not only sent by Heaven but was sent by a *kindness* from Heaven... Because assimilation and intermarriage are worse than death... And the German Jews and others ignored the Torah teachers and refused to desist from their mad race into assimilation, the Nazis were sent to prevent them and rescue them before they were swallowed by the nations." I do not understand how this rabbi from Baltimore, who was ordained by Yeshiva College in New York and went on to study at the Slabodka Yeshiva in Lithuania, has the chutzpah to blame the Holocaust on sins of the Jews.

A unique version of the theory that the Holocaust occurred because of sin is presented by Ignaz Maybaum (1897-1976), a prominent Reform rabbi from London, originally from Berlin, who spent six weeks in a Nazi concentration camp and whose mother died in Terezin and his two sisters and other relatives in Auschwitz. In his 1965 book *The Face of God after Auschwitz,* he claims that the Holocaust happened not because of the sins of the Jews but because of the sins of others. He speaks of the Holocaust as the third *Hurban* ("catastrophe"), the destruction of the first temple of Solomon being the first *Hurban,* and the destruction of the second temple being the second *Hurban.* He claims that a *Hurban* is the work of God which "thrust[s] the history of mankind into a new chapter." In the first two *Hurbans,* the Jews suffered for their own sins. However, the Holocaust occurred for the sins of humanity. He views Hitler as an instrument of God. "The innocent who died in Auschwitz, not for the sake of their own sins, but because of the sins of others..."

Maybaum tells us that we should never stop speaking about the six million Jews who perished during the third Hurban, but at the same time, he wants us to remember that although Eastern European Jewry was destroyed, two-thirds of the Jews of the world survived.

Richard Rubenstein

The most radical theological response to the Holocaust is that of Rabbi Richard L. Rubenstein, a Conservative rabbi. He had a transforming experience in 1961 when he had a two-hour conversation with pastor Heinrich Gruber (1891–1975), a strong opponent of Nazism who was arrested by the Gestapo and testified against Adolf Eichmann. At the time that Rubenstein met Gruber, he was a pastor at a church in East Berlin. He told Rubenstein that "it had been God's will to send Adolph Hitler to exterminate Europe's Jews." When Rubenstein heard that, he experienced a crisis of faith and said: "I recognized that Gruber was not an anti-Semite and that his assertion that the God of the Covenant was and is the ultimate author of the great events of Israel's history was no different from the faith of any traditional Jew." At that moment, Rubenstein felt that the Holocaust must, in some sense, express the will of God and found it obscene that God could have inflicted Auschwitz on His people. Rubenstein wrote, "I have had to decide whether to affirm the existence of a God who inflicts Auschwitz on his guilty people or to insist that nothing the Jews did make them more deserving of Auschwitz than any other people. That Auschwitz was in no sense a punishment and that a God who could or would inflict such punishment does not exist... I have done so as a rabbi and a theologian in the full knowledge that my choice has been rejected by my people. Nevertheless, I would rather be rejected by my people than affirm their guilt at Auschwitz." Rubenstein concludes that it is no longer possible for him to believe in a traditional concept of God.

Emil Fackenheim

The first person to whom I told my own story of survival in Eastern Europe was Emil Fackenheim, perhaps the most prolific radical writer for whom the Holocaust brings a new revelation. In addition to the 613 commandments in Judaism, Fackenheim insisted that there now must be a 614th commandment, "Not to despair of God and not to despair of man." Fackenheim was arrested by the Nazis on the night of November 9, 1938, known as *Kristall Nacht* ("the night of the broken glass"), and was sent to the Sachsenhausen concentration camp. He came to Grinnell in 1972 and spoke on "The Commanding Voice of Auschwitz." In his talk, Fackenheim stressed that the voice of Auschwitz commands that Jews are forbidden to give up on Judaism because that would hand Hitler a posthumous victory. I feel that it is essential to quote him at some length since this passage that cites the commanding voice of Auschwitz is an important passage of post-Holocaust theology:

What does the voice of Auschwitz command?

> Jews are forbidden to hand Hitler posthumous victories. They are commanded to survive as Jews, lest the Jewish people perish. They are commanded to remember the victims of Auschwitz, lest their memory perish. They are forbidden to despair of man and his world, and to escape into either cynicism or otherworldliness, lest they cooperate in delivering the world over to the forces of Auschwitz. Finally, they are forbidden to despair of the God of Israel, lest Judaism perish... One possibility, however, is wholly unthinkable. A Jew may not respond to Hitler's attempt to destroy Judaism by himself cooperating in its destruction. In ancient times, the unthinkable Jewish sin was idolatry. Today, it is to respond to Hitler by doing his work.

The most significant fact about the Holocaust for Fackenheim is what it does not have in common with other cases of genocide, namely, that at the Wannsee Conference, which took place on January 20, 1942, fifteen high-ranking members of the Nazi Party decided that not a single Jew must stay alive. Every Jew was to be murdered. At this beautiful place outside of Berlin, they came to implement what they called the "final solution of the Jewish question." Fackenheim and Wiesel knew that millions of Christians were also murdered by the Nazis. But they claimed that only the Jews were singled out for complete eradication. Wiesel said, "Not all victims were Jews, but all Jews were victims."

Now that I have done a brief review of the theologians who see the Holocaust as an unprecedented event, I turn to the views of those who feel that it is one more tragic event in Jewish history. Many Jewish thinkers have serious problems with the Holocaust theologians like Rubenstein, Fackenheim, and Wiesel. For some Orthodox thinkers, Auschwitz is unique in the magnitude of its horror but not in the problem it presents for religious faith. Some Orthodox Jews refuse to take part in an official annual day to commemorate the Holocaust because they feel that the Holocaust was not a unique event. In stark contrast to Fackenheim's views are those of Michael Wyschogrod, one of the most respected Orthodox thinkers of our time. In a well-known, penetrating article titled "Faith and the Holocaust," he writes:

> Israel's faith has always centered on the saving acts of God: the election, the Exodus, the Temple, and the Messiah. However more prevalent destruction was in the history of Israel, the acts of destruction were enshrined in minor fast days while those of redemption became the joyous proclamations of the Passover and Tabernacles, of Hanukkah and Purim. The God of Israel is a redeeming God; this is the only message we are authorized to proclaim, however much it may not seem so to the eyes of non-belief. Should the Holocaust cease to be peripheral to the faith of Israel, should it enter the Holy of Holies and become the dominant voice that

Israel hears, it could not but be a demonic voice that it would be hearing. There is no salvation to be extracted from the Holocaust, no faltering Judaism can be revived by it, no new reason for the continuation of the Jewish people can be found in it. If there is hope after the Holocaust, it is because to those who believe, the voices of the Prophets speak more loudly than did Hitler, and because the divine promise sweeps over the crematoria and silences the voice of Auschwitz.

Professor Jacob Neusner, a Conservative rabbi and one of the best-known scholars of Judaic studies, is also critical of the Holocaust thinkers. In his article "The Implications of the Holocaust," he states: "I claim there is no implication—none for Judaic theology, none for Jewish community life—which was not present before 1933. In fact, Judaic piety has all along known how to respond to a disaster."

Abraham Joshua Heschel: Living with the Holocaust

Very little has been written about the reaction of Abraham Joshua Heschel to the Holocaust. This may be because he did not write a separate study on the Holocaust and because in his written work, he tended to stress one point of view and then another point of view. On certain issues, Heschel's perspectives are extremely complex. This is especially the case in writing about the Holocaust. Even today, for example, more than forty years after his death, Heschel scholars are deeply divided on whether he believed in divine omnipotence, a God who is all-powerful, and thus whether he believed that God might have been able to prevent the Holocaust from happening.

Although Heschel did not focus directly on the Holocaust, we do find in his writings many statements from which we can discern its profound impact on his life. In a 1967 interview at Notre Dame University, he stated:

"I am really a person who is in anguish. I can't forget what I have seen and been through. Auschwitz and Hiroshima never leave my mind. Nothing can be the same after that." Heschel further claims that "Auschwitz is in our veins. It abides in the throbbing of our hearts. It burns in our imagination. It trembles in our conscience."

In one of his most important essays, "No Religion is an Island," Heschel defines himself as a survivor:

> "I am a brand plucked from the fire in which my people were burned to death. I am a brand plucked from the fire of an altar [to] Satan on which millions of lives were exterminated to evil's greater glory..."

We now also know that during Heschel's first five years in America (1940–1945), he made many efforts, unfortunately in vain, to rally support for intervention that would save European Jews. What did he do when no one listened to him? He went to a synagogue to pray, fast, recite psalms, and weep. Like many other survivors, Heschel struggled with God his entire life, a struggle that continued to the very end and, I believe, was never fully resolved. In one of his most extraordinary talks, which has been reprinted numerous times, Heschel cried out to God, "Where is God? Why didst Thou not halt the trains loaded with Jews being led to slaughter? It is so hard to rear a child, to nourish and to educate. Why dost Thou make it so easy to kill?

On the one hand, a reading of Heschel shows that he blamed the Holocaust on humanity: "For the Holocaust did not take place suddenly. It was in the making for several generations. It had its origin in a lie; that the Jew was responsible for all social ills, for all personal frustrations. Decimate the Jews, and all problems would be solved. The Holocaust was initiated by demonic thoughts, savage words." Clearly, here, he blames the Holocaust on the depravity of human beings. It was they who created the gas chambers.

Several of Heschel's friends and students were puzzled that he did not write more directly about the Holocaust. Arthur Green tells us how difficult it was to be a follower of Heschel. At a time when he was reading Elie Wiesel's book *Night*, in which Wiesel speaks of God as dying on the gallows of Auschwitz, and Richard Rubenstein was saying that it was blasphemy to continue to believe in divine providence, Heschel was writing on Jewish ways of encountering God's presence. Emil Fackenheim, who was a great admirer of Heschel, points out that, like Martin Buber, Heschel "said little about the Holocaust—and that little with great reticence." Fackenheim came to understand that Heschel did not formulate a new theology of the Holocaust because it did not pose a new theological problem for him. And Heschel's students came to understand that his stand against the war in Vietnam, his deep involvement with Martin Luther King, and his action for Soviet Jewry were his response to the Holocaust. Heschel wanted to find ways to help God heal the world rather than to speculate about how to justify God. For Heschel, God needs partners; he does not need our recommendation.

Heschel's experience of the Holocaust is certainly one of the reasons for his social activism. He lived in Germany from 1927 to 1938, where he experienced racism and often pointed out how violence towards others begins with words. His daughter Susannah Heschel tells us, "He used to remind us that the Holocaust did not begin with the building of crematoria, and Hitler did not come to power with tanks and guns; it all began with uttering evil words, with defamation, language, and propaganda." Heschel did not blame God. He said that God did not do it. Man did it. For Heschel, God is a God of pathos who cares and participates in human suffering and, therefore, was there with the victims in the Holocaust.

Another reading of Heschel suggests that he could not totally give up the idea that God could have intervened in the Holocaust. We are now touching on one of the most critical and controversial issues. There is serious disagreement among scholars as to whether Heschel rejects the idea of divine omnipotence. In his classic work *God in Search of Man,* Heschel tells us that God "combines justice with omnipotence." Later in this same work, Heschel does not seem to question the omnipotence of God, stating that "the omnipotence of God is not always perceptible." I agree with John Merkle, who, when interpreting Heschel's view, says that "God's presence in history should not be understood as God's dominance of history." But I am not convinced that Heschel gave up on the idea that God could intervene in history to help shape its course. Merkle never suggests that Heschel rejects this idea, but he does suggest that Heschel, at least toward the end of his life, came to reject the idea of divine omnipotence. Although he makes a strong case for this, basing his argument upon Heschel's claims that "the idea of divine omnipotence… is a non-Jewish idea" and that "God's mercy is too great to permit the innocent to suffer" but that "there are forces that interfere with God's mercy, with God's power," I believe that Heschel never completely resolved the issue of divine omnipotence.

Heschel, who, like many other East European Jews of his time, devoted a good part of his life to the study of the Talmud, the central sacred text of Jewish learning. A core teaching of the Talmud, with which Heschel was certainly familiar, is that "everything is in the hands of heaven except for fear of heaven" (Berakhot 33b). I fully agree with Gordon Tucker's nonliteral translation of this passage as "God can do anything except make us believe in God." This important passage from the Talmud helps us understand the incredible dilemma that confronted Heschel, who believed in a God of pathos, a God who suffers with the suffering of human beings, who intervened to liberate the children of Israel from Egyptian bondage but did not intervene similarly during the Holocaust.

For Heschel, as I understand him, the limitation of God's power in history is self-imposed. Heschel's wrestling with God is precise since God does not always interfere in the world during times of great suffering. From the time that Heschel was a young man, he confronted God and would not exonerate Him for the world's pain. Human beings are responsible, but that does not let God off the hook from ultimate responsibility. I am still struggling with my last statement because I am aware of Heschel's close affinity to the second-century sage, Rabbi Akiva, who "believed that it is better to limit belief in God's power than to dampen faith in God's mercy." However, on this issue, I think that Heschel comes closer to the view of Akiva's contemporary, Rabbi Ishmael, who believed in an omnipotent God. Let me explain.

From Heschel's early book of Yiddish poems, *The Ineffable Name of God: Man*, it is clear that Heschel could not adjust himself to the evil in the world. He stands in the tradition of Abraham, of Job, and of his great Hasidic ancestor

Levi Yitzhak of Berditchev, who is known for challenging God to bring an end to suffering.

In his poem called "Help," Heschel writes:

> *The desolate call to You and You don't come.*
> *So, send me, and any others, You might choose.*
> *I can't curse as justly as did Jeremiah.*
> *People are poor, weak; and it seems to me*
> *that their guilt is Yours;*
> *their sins, Your crimes.*
> *You are meant to help here, Oh God!*
> *But You are silent, while needs shriek.*
> *So, help me to help! I'll fulfill Your duty,*
> *pay Your debts.*

We know that Heschel was deeply influenced by Menahem Mendel, the Kotzker Rebbe. Heschel said: "Throughout my entire life, the words of the Kotzker Rebbe burned within me." For Heschel, as for the Kotzker, "A man of flesh and blood was simply not meant to comprehend the divine response to the deepest of human problems. Divine secrets were not compatible with the human intellect." Is there, then, any purpose in asking these terrifying questions to which we will not get the answers? Both the Kotzker's and Heschel's answer is "Yes." It is true that no answer can be gained by human beings, but we must persist in our search. The Kotzker locked himself in a room for the last twenty years of his life to struggle with God. I'm grateful that Heschel continued his struggle by living among us.

I have spoken of Heschel's responses to the Holocaust, and not his answers, because I agree with the following statement of Elie Wiesel, with which I believe Heschel would concur: "The survivors...Are aware of the fact that God's presence at Treblinka or Maidanek—or, for that matter, His absence—poses a problem which will remain forever insoluble... Perhaps someday someone will explain how, on the level of man, Auschwitz was possible; but on the level of God, it will forever remain the most disturbing of mysteries." Mordecai Kaplan (1881–1983), the great Lithuanian American philosopher of Judaism who founded the Reconstructionist Movement, had a vision of Judaism that was radically different from Heschel's. Yet when it came to the Holocaust, he was in full agreement with Heschel that there was no answer. He said, "Not a single one of the numerous theodicies or attempts of thinkers to reconcile the goodness of God with the existence of evil has ever proved convincing."

Let me end with a story. "One writer on the Holocaust records that in his research, he met a rabbi who had been through the camps and who miraculously seemed unscarred. He could still laugh. 'How,' he asked him, 'could you see what you saw and still have faith? Did you have no questions?' The rabbi replied, 'Of course I had questions. But I said to myself: if you ever ask those questions, they are such powerful questions that God will send you a personal invitation to Heaven to give you the answers. And I preferred to be here on earth with the questions than in Heaven with the answers.'" That, too, is a theology of a kind, with roots deep in the Biblical tradition.

Chapter 2

Paths to Jewish Holiness

"And ye shall be unto Me a kingdom of priests, and a holy nation" (Exodus 9:6).

You shall be holy, for I the Lord Your God am holy" (Leviticus 19:2).

When I recently told a rabbi that I was writing an essay on Jewish saints, he was somewhat puzzled. I am not surprised. When Jews think about saints, they usually think of Christianity. They think of the Catholic process of beatification and canonization by which the Church declares a person to be a saint. In Judaism, there is no official religious body that can recognize someone as a saint. But there are saints in the Jewish tradition. When a person lives a holy, pious life, the Jewish community may come to recognize that human being as a saint. In the Jewish tradition, a saint, or a spiritual master, may be called a *talmid hakham* ("disciple of the wise"), *tzaddik* ("a righteous person"), or *hasid* ("pious person"). There are also other terms for the spiritually elite in the Jewish tradition, such as *gaon* ("genius") and *gadol hador* ("the Torah leader of the generation").

But how does Judaism define a saint? I would define a saint as a person who views *Imitatio Dei* as the ultimate purpose of life[1] and who is totally committed to the following two commandments from the Torah: "You must love the Lord your God with all your heart and with all your soul and with all your might" (Deuteronomy VI, 4) and "Love your neighbor as yourself" (Leviticus XIX, 17).[2] The test of a holy life is the willingness to give up one's life for the sake of the commandments. Saints are always ready to die for God.

Because the Jewish tradition places such a strong emphasis on study, on the mind, the Jewish saint will most likely come from the ranks of the *talmid hakhamim*, a sage who has astonishingly mastered the Torah and attained great stature in the community.[3] Classical Judaism sees such a person as the ideal because the Torah is believed to be the word of God, and the study of the Torah is seen as "holiness in words." Study, it is said, not only leads to paradise; it is paradise. By studying the Torah, we can discern the will of God and fulfill all the *mitzvot* ("commandments").[4] The person who submits to God's will and fulfills both the ritual *mitzvot* and the ethical *mitzvot* becomes holy.

The Jewish tradition sees Rabbi Elijah ben Solomon of Vilna (1720–1797), who is known as the Vilna Gaon and who studied Torah eighteen hours a day, as the ideal spiritual master in the Jewish tradition. He was known as *ha-Gaon he-Hasid*.[5]

Some Jews, who are not great scholars, may also be recognized as saints because of their intense love of God, their humility, or because they may be blessed with divine inspiration, which gives them special power to influence God. The greatest challenge to the classical conception of a Jewish saint was the Baal Shem Tov (1700–1760), the founder of the Hasidic movement. He did not come from the ranks of the *talmid hakhamim,* and he was not known for his extraordinary knowledge of the Torah. The Baal Shem Tov gave greater emphasis to the heart than to the mind. He himself was a teacher of small children and a laborer who spent a great deal of time meditating in the forest rather than in the study hall. For the Baal Shem Tov, ecstatic, joyful, and heartfelt prayer superseded the study of the Torah to cleave to God.

The Baal Shem Tov was viewed by his followers as the ideal saint, the ideal master, the great *tzaddik*. His followers began to emphasize the doctrine of the *tzaddik* as an intermediary between themselves and God. According to this doctrine, if we want to become attached to God, we must attach ourselves to the *tzaddik*, whose thoughts are entirely God-centered. According to Louis Jacobs, the Hasidic master Elimelech of Lizensk (1717–1787) claimed that the *tzaddik* "brings man near to God and he brings down God's grace from heaven to earth."[6] We should not be surprised, therefore, that the Gaon of Vilna banned the Hasidic movement.

Moses Maimonides (1135–1204), the great Jewish philosopher, of whom it is said "From Moses to Moses there was none like Moses," distinguishes between two types of ideal people: the *hakham*, the sage, and the *hasid*, the saint. Rabbi Jonathan Sacks claims that Maimonides favors the sage over the saint because *"the sage is concerned with the perfection of society. The saint is concerned with the perfection of self."*[7] This is a useful distinction, but it does not always work so neatly in reality. The greatest Jewish sage, the Vilna Gaon, is also seen as a great saint. The sage from Vilna devoted so much time to the study of the Torah that it left him little time to become involved in the affairs of his community. He never accepted a rabbinic position.

> The Gaon's way of life, as portrayed by his sons and his students, was characterized by the maximum channeling of the powers of body and soul to one exclusive goal: the study of the Torah. In practice, the Gaon understood absolute devotion to Torah study as one side of the coin; the other side was the value of asceticism and withdrawal from society as a guiding principle and way of life... [T]he Gaon saw the main significance of asceticism in its channeling of the majority of an individual's physical and spiritual resources toward the purpose of Torah study. He, therefore, particularly stressed the value of separation from the society of other people, as social contact brings in its wake the loss of time from Torah study, while isolation from society assists in the constancy of study.[8]

In his final book, *A Passion for Truth*, Rabbi Abraham Joshua Heschel points out the affinity that the major Hasidic leader Rabbi Mendel of Kotzk, known as the Kotzker, had for the Gaon of Vilna by citing the following passage about the Gaon:

> The Gaon would not receive people in order to save all his time for his studies. When his sister came to see him after an absence of twelve years, he said to his attendant, "tell her we'll see each other in the next world. I have no time for such meetings here."[9]

Heschel claims that the Kotzker had a somewhat similar view: "Both lived in solitude, cut off from the world."[10] In his excellent article "Ascetical Aspects of Ancient Judaism," Steven D. Fraade, professor at Yale University, states:

"If the central religious obligation is that of the study of Torah (and attachment to God through it), then worldly preoccupations such as family are bound to be distracting for reasons of time, energy, and purity."[11] Here we can see the strong ascetic strain in the Jewish tradition, which we will find in Moses Hayyim Luzzatto's path to holiness.

In contrast, the Baal Shem Tov, who revealed himself as a spiritual master when he was thirty-six years old, did not believe that to live a spiritual life, it is necessary to divorce oneself from this world. He stressed a passage from the prophet Isaiah that "the whole world is full of His presence" (Isaiah VI, 1). Even more central to his teaching is his interpretation of the phrase from Proverbs "In all your ways know God" (Prov 3:6). For the Baal Shem Tov, people have different paths to God. Study may not be the path for everyone; each person needs to find the right path for himself. The Baal Shem Tov felt that the highest peak of spiritual living is attained through immersion in everyday life. Heschel's statement on the Baal Shem Tov helps us see the contrast between the Baal Shem Tov and the Gaon of Vilna:

> Before the Baal Shem's time, pious Jews felt that to be close to God, the body must be chastised; one must fast and scourge oneself. Bodily enjoyment was considered despicable; sexual pleasures filled them with revulsion. But the Baal Shem and his followers held that all delights come from Eden. "A longing for things material is an instrument by which one may approach the love of God; even through coarse desires, one may come to love the Creator." Lust, desire, evil inclination, all should be elevated, not uprooted.[12]

"For the Baal Shem Tov," says Heschel, "saintliness and worldliness are not mutually exclusive."[13]

For the Mithnagdim, the traditional Jews who opposed the Hasidim, Hasidic beliefs seem to blur the distinction between the sacred and profane. Especially troubling to them and their leader, the Gaon of Vilna, was the Hasidic sanctification of food and drink. The Gaon of Vilna discouraged excessive eating even on the Sabbath. One of his students recounts the following conversation:

> When I spoke of this matter before my teacher, the Gaon, of blessed memory, he told me that he had a general principle that even though it is a *mitzvah* to eat and drink on the Sabbath, it is also a *mitzvah* to study Torah on the Sabbath. It is then much better to increase one's study than to increase one's eating and drinking. For increasing study will help develop study habits, and study is a *mitzvah* at all other times as well. On the other hand, eating on the Sabbath will lead to a greater appetite on weekdays as well.[14]

It may seem that the Mithnagdic and the Hassidic conceptions of the saint cannot be reconciled. But as I will demonstrate in the third section, there is a modern-day saint who combines the virtues of both models of the saint.

Moses Hayyim Luzzatto

How does one become a saint? The best description of a path to holiness in the classical Jewish tradition can be found in the writings of the great Jewish mystic and ethical writer from Italy, Moses Hayyim Luzzatto (1707–1746). His *Mesillat Yesharim* ("The Path of the Upright"), arguably the most influential Jewish book on ethics, presents a systematic, step-by-step eightfold path on how to attain holiness: "Holiness is of a twofold nature; it begins as a quality of the service rendered to God, but it ends as a reward for such service. It is at first a type of spiritual effort and then a kind of spiritual gift. A man must first strive to be holy, and then he is endowed with holiness."[15]

Luzzatto's work is actually an investigation into a single teaching from the second century Rabbi Phinehas ben Yair, who stated: "The knowledge of Torah leads to watchfulness, watchfulness to zeal, zeal to cleanness, cleanness to abstinence, abstinence to purity, purity to saintliness, saintliness to humility, humility to fear of sin, and fear of sin to holiness."[16] Luzzatto transformed his hierarchy of qualities into a detailed guide to how man could perfect himself.

Luzzatto based his arguments on the belief that human beings because they are imbued with a divine soul, cannot be satisfied with anything that can be found in this world. Human beings were created to enjoy the world to come. Luzzatto writes: "Likewise if thou were to offer the soul all the pleasures of the world, she would remain indifferent to them because she belongs to a higher order of existence (Koheleth R. to 6.7)"[17] Therefore, this world should be viewed only as a path to fulfillment in the world to come.

1. Watchfulness

Luzzatto teaches: "All of man's strivings should be directed toward the Creator, blessed be He. A man should have no other purpose in whatever he does, be it great or small, than to draw nigh to God and to break down all separating walls, that is, all things of a material nature, between himself and his Master, so that he may be drawn to God as iron to a magnet."[18]

Following Rabbi Phinehas ben Yair's model, Luzzatto explains that the first step to holiness begins with watchfulness; that is, taking great care to avoid the evil inclination inside oneself. Only by studying the Torah and taking time to consider its ethical lessons can one avoid the evil inclination: "In fine, a man should at all times consider carefully what course to pursue so as to conform with the laws of the Torah. He should also set aside stated periods when he may contemplate in solitude."[19] Watchfulness is endangered by three factors: "The first is a preoccupation with worldly affairs; the second is frivolity and levity; the third is the society of evil companions."[20] All three could compromise one's intent to live by the code of the Torah. Of these three, Luzzatto is most concerned about the danger of involvement in worldly affairs, which he considers the most common enemy, but also the easiest to overcome. At the same time, he is opposed to severe asceticism. He realizes that a human being must devote a certain amount of time to making a livelihood, though devoting one's life to materialism would not deliver lasting bliss or salvation.

2. Zeal

Watchfulness pertains to the negative commandments, while zeal pertains to the positive ones. He who is watchful merely avoids sin; he who is zealous also does good. Zeal means a commitment to do the mitzvot whenever possible. To acquire this commitment is no simple task; it requires great strength. Luzzatto writes: "It should be borne in mind that it is the nature of man to be inert and that the earthiness of the physical element in him acts as a weight upon him. Man, therefore, seeks to avoid all toil and effort.

Accordingly, a man who desires the privilege of worshiping the Creator, blessed be He, must be able to prevail over his own nature, and act with strength and energy."[21]

3. Cleanness

According to Luzzatto, "The quality of cleanness consists in being free from the evil traits as well as from sin."[22] Cleanness of soul is higher than watchfulness and zeal because the person who acquires the stages of watchfulness and zeal only succeeds in keeping his evil inclination in check, but he does not eradicate it. The person who has attained the higher stage of cleanness is beyond the evil inclination—beyond lust, beyond temptation. As a person becomes clean, the fire of lust will die out in his heart and its cessation will bring about a longing for the divine: "The true way to acquire the trait of spiritual cleanness is to read assiduously the words of our Sages, both their legal enactments and their ethical exhortations."[23] Luzzatto believes that most people are only capable of reaching the stage of cleanness, but only a few can become saints.

4. Abstinence

The stage of abstinence marks the way to saintliness. The great enemy of abstinence is the craving and attachment to the pleasures of the world. The senses are indeed powerful antagonists to the greatest of men and women. The eyes of human beings are captivated by things that are outwardly beautiful and charming. It was these perceptions that "lead to man's original sin, as scripture testifies."[24]

The way to attain abstinence is by realizing the true nature of pleasures. Luzzatto believes that pleasures are useless, worthless, and transient. Once a human being has attained abstinence, he will no longer be allured by physical pleasures, "for he will know that he may enjoy in this world only those things without which he can't live."[25]

5. Purity

Purity follows abstinence. The essence of purity is the perfecting of one's heart and one's thoughts. Above all, to be pure is to attain perfect worship: "It can be called perfect only when it is pure and is rendered for no reason except that of serving God."[26] Before one reaches this stage, one must realize that human glory is vanity, and one must view ambition as merely striving after the wind. Purity is zeal stripped of ego. It is higher than cleanness because cleanness involves only eradicating the evil inclination, while purity involves the actual performance of mitzvot. By meditating for many hours, one prepares oneself for the performance of a mitzvah and, in so doing, becomes one with it. Only at this point "will he perform his religious duties with no thought of the praise he might win; his mind will then be directed wholly toward his Master. He alone is our glory, our good, and our perfection."[27]

6. Saintliness

Luzzatto compares the saint to a lover who is always ready to do more than required. As a lover of God, the aim is always to give happiness to one's Creator. Luzzatto devotes four chapters to saintliness, placing great stress on wisdom and the centrality of the study of the Torah. He states: "Saintliness should be reared upon great wisdom and upon the adjustment of conduct to the aims worthy of the truly wise. Only the wise can truly grasp the nature of saintliness; as our Sages said, 'The ignorant man cannot be saintly.'"[28] The need to attain wisdom by studying Torah day and night may be a major reason why Luzzatto, who clearly favors the world to come over this world, is opposed to prolonged fasting and other ascetic practices. Luzzatto was surely familiar with the rabbinic view that "a Torah scholar may not fast because he is detracting from the work of heaven."[29]

7. Humility

A saint has reached the stage of humility when he does not think of himself at all. His whole being is concerned with the glory of God and submission to God's will. Constant humility can only be achieved through reflection and training. This means habituating oneself in humbleness until humility is an implicit part of being.

8. Fear of Sin

By fear of sin, Luzzatto does not mean only the fear of punishment but also a sense of awe for the glory of God. This sense of awe is the inevitable result of submitting one's entire self to the will of God. Since Luzzatto believed that the fate of the world depended on our conduct, fearing sin was equivalent to fearing the destruction of the world.

9. Holiness

While great commitment can allow man to ascend through the first seven stages, the final stage of Luzzatto's path—holiness—is beyond the effort of human beings alone. He writes:

> But since it is impossible for a man to attain this status through his own efforts—for he is, after all, only a physical being, mere flesh, and blood—holiness has to be finally granted to him as a gift...

> [I]t is the Holy One, blessed be He, who leads man in the path he has chosen, and who imparts to him some of His own holiness, thereby rendering him holy... [T]he man who is holy, he who is always in communion with his God, ... is accounted as though he beheld the presence of the Lord, notwithstanding that he is still in this world.[30]

Judaism, as well as Christianity and Islam, are sometimes characterized as religions of faith, in contrast to Asian religions, which are said to be religions of experience. It is claimed that the Jew is required only to have faith in God and God's revelation. A reading of Luzzatto reveals that the saint not only has faith but that he has real experiences of God in this life. Luzzatto claims that faith in God combined with the will to holiness can lead one step-by-step "until there is poured upon him a spirit from on high and the name of the Creator, blessed be He, will abide within him as it does within all holy things."[31]

Like the Buddhist eightfold path, Luzzatto's path begins with watchfulness and, as one continues to struggle on this path, one may reach the stage of fear of sin. When one reaches that stage, the holy spirit may then descend, and one attains holiness. Once one is granted holiness by God, claims Luzzatto, one has the power to resurrect the dead.

Mesillat Yesharim became an important ethical text for both the Mithnagdim and the Hasidim. The Hasidim, who elevated prayer over Torah study and made *devekut* ("communion with God") their central goal, felt a strong affinity for Luzzatto's holy path because they felt it leads to *devekut*. At the same time, the Gaon of Vilna is said to have stated that he could not find a superfluous word in the first seven chapters of *Mesillat Yesharim*—and were Luzzatto still alive, he would walk across Europe to study with him.

Rabbi Israel Salanter and the Musar Movement

But Luzzatto's greatest influence was among the devotees of the Musar movement, an ethical self-perfection movement founded in Vilnius by Rabbi Israel Salanter (1810–1883). Salanter, one of the most influential Orthodox thinkers of the nineteenth century, felt a strong affinity for Luzzatto, stressing that the primary goal of a human being is to strive for ethical perfection. Rabbi Dov Katz, a third-generation disciple of Salanter, wrote: "His avowed aim in life was the attainment of spiritual perfection. He regarded ethical perfection as the entire purpose for being on earth."[32] Salanter believed that "It was more difficult to change a single character trait than to master the entire Talmud."[33] Yet for him, this was a task that must be undertaken, and that would ultimately lead to the transformation of the individual:

Yet let no one say: What God has made cannot be changed. He, may He be blessed, has infused an evil drive in me; how can I ever hope to eradicate it? It is not so. Man's drives can be subdued and even changed... It is within his power to conquer his evil nature and prevent its functioning, and also to change his nature to good by study and training.[34]

In the preface to his book *Mesillat Yesharim*, Luzzatto complains that people are devoting too much time to the study of Jewish law and are not paying sufficient attention to the study of Musar: "There are but few who study the nature of the love and the fear of God, of communion, or any other phase of saintliness."[35] This captures precisely the view of Salanter, who made the study of Musar texts central to achieving a holy life and who helped Luzzatto's *Mesillat Yesharim* become the most widely used basic text among the *yeshivot* of Lithuania.[36]

At the beginning of the twenty-first century, there are only a few *Yeshivot* in the United States and Israel that emphasize Musar in their curriculum. Although there are four English translations of *Mesillat Yesharim,* the Jewish world as a whole is not familiar with the Musar movement and its preeminent ethical text.[37]

Abraham Joshua Heschel: A Jewish Saint of the Twentieth Century

I, along with many other Jews and Christians, regard Rabbi Abraham Joshua Heschel (1907–1972) to be the Jewish saint of the twentieth century. His first student in America, Rabbi Samuel Dresner, claimed that Heschel was "*zaddik hador*," the saint of our generation.[38] For Heschel's disciple, Byron Sherwin, "Abraham Joshua Heschel was a jewel from God's treasure chest."[39] Christians speak of Heschel as the most significant spiritual writer of our time and often call him a prophet.[40] I view Heschel's *God in Search of Man* as a modern equivalent of Luzzatto's Jewish path to holiness. Heschel's book can be seen as "a way of developing sensitivity to God and attachment to His presence."[41]

God in Search of Man is devoted to three interrelated aspects of a Jewish path through which contemporary Jews can open themselves to God or, more precisely, through which we can respond to God, who, according to Heschel, needs human beings. In Heschel's words, "There are three starting points of contemplation about God; three trails that lead to Him. The first is the way of sensing the presence of God in the world in things; the second is the way of sensing His presence in the Bible; the third is the way of sensing His presence in sacred deeds."[42]

Heschel has been called the philosopher of wonder because he believed that awareness of the Divine begins with wonder. For Heschel, radical amazement can help us to experience the realm of the ineffable. Heschel takes as his task in the first path to tell us how to sense wonder and awe, how to see the holy in the everyday, to see that all of life is sacred.

The second of Heschel's paths to God is encountering God through the words of the Bible. Heschel asserts that the Bible is the ideal path through which Jews can encounter God. However, mere Biblical study will not disclose the presence of God. We must approach the Bible with our whole being. We must also cultivate certain virtues, such as humility and truthfulness, and attempt to rid ourselves of pride, pettiness, and falsehood.

In Heschel's third path, the way of sensing God's presence in sacred deeds, he claims that modern human beings who have difficulty with the first two paths, who still can't open their eyes, have a final alternative. Heschel presents a most challenging and provocative claim. He contends that performing the mitzvot, the commandments, is not merely our response to the demands of God. They may also serve as a path *to* God. The fact that contemporary human beings are callous to the mystery of existence and detached from the Biblical tradition leads Heschel to say that the way through deeds may be our last hope.

The significance that Heschel attaches to sacred deeds becomes apparent when he states, "A Jew is asked to take a leap of action rather than a leap of thought. He is asked to surpass his needs, to do more than he understands in order to understand more than he does. In carrying out the words of the Torah, he is ushered into the presence of spiritual meaning. Through the ecstasy of deeds, he learns to be certain of the hereness of God. Right living is a way of right thinking."[43]

Further along, Heschel explains more fully why the Jew is asked to take a leap of action: "The mitzvah is a supreme source of religious insight and experience. The way to God is a way of God, and the mitzvah is a way of God, a way where the self-evidence of the holy is disclosed...A mitzvah is where God and man meet...To meet Him means to come upon an inner certainty of His realness, upon an awareness of His will. Such a meaning, such presence we experience in deeds."[44]

There are clearly major affinities as well as differences between the works of Luzzatto and Heschel. Luzzatto was writing during a time when, for most Jews, God was a reality. Luzzatto's aim was to lead ordinary Jews to saintliness. Heschel, on the other hand, wrote during a time when the belief in a supernatural concept of God was no longer a reality for many Jews. He aimed to convince Jews that awareness of God's reality would help lead them to a more spiritual, holy life.

Luzzatto's path, which stresses personal transformation, is more otherworldly than Heschel's path, which is deeply concerned with the everyday. Because of the intense effort that is necessary to attain saintliness, there is little time in Luzzatto's path for one to be involved in the community. Heschel, on the other hand, became involved in a number of compelling social and political issues of his day.

Judaism commands love of both God and neighbor. The question that has often been asked is: Does love of God take priority over love of neighbor? I would argue that that is the case for Luzzatto. For Heschel, who always attempted to create a balance between the polarities in Judaism, human beings come first. Heschel observed, "Every human being is made in the image of God. Therefore, if we are serving our fellow human beings, in a very real sense, we are serving God as well."[45] This is how Heschel characterized a saint: "A saint was he who did not know how it is possible not to love, not to help, not to be sensitive to the anxiety of others."[46]

With his attention to the world and the Divine, Heschel combined the hallowing of the everyday of the Baal Shem Tov with the brilliant scholarship of the Gaon of Vilna and the ethical fervor of Israel Salanter. Heschel described—and lived—a modern path to sainthood.

Chapter 3

Heschel's View of Religious Diversity

A few weeks before he died in 1972, Abraham Joshua Heschel left the following message for young people: "And above all, remember that the meaning of life is to build a life as if it were a work of art. You're not a machine. And you are young. Start working on this great work of art called your own existence."[47]

If one's life is meant to be a work of art, then Heschel's life was a masterpiece. He was one of the most significant religious thinkers of the last century who, at the same time, was deeply engaged in the social issues of his day. He was a passionately committed Jew and an "apostle to the gentiles" who was revered by many Christians and considered a tzaddik, a saint, by many Jews. He was a major figure in both the peace movement opposed to the Vietnam War and the civil rights movement, and he worked vigorously to help Jews suffering in the Soviet Union.

What stood out about Heschel was his ability to speak as a Jew, but a Jew who could communicate beyond the boundaries of his own religious tradition. The Catholic theologian John Merkle said it best: "In his own life and works, Abraham Joshua Heschel revealed the supreme importance of God as well as what it is like to live with faith in God."[48]

In his essay "Heschel's Impact on Catholic-Jewish Relations," Eugene Fisher, former executive secretary of the Secretariat for Catholic-Jewish Relations of the National Conference of Catholic Bishops, writes:

> Heschel's work and life, of course, were particularly profound in their influence on American Catholics of my generation. His thought spiritually enriched us as his courageous deeds—whether marching for civil rights or against the Vietnam War—prophetically challenged us. To many of us in the Catholic community active in the 1960s, Abraham Joshua Heschel, along with Thomas Merton and Dorothy Day, were perceived as no less than contemporary prophets, searing our souls and enflaming our vision with God's hope for a better humanity. Through him, we learned to understand, to feel, what it means to say that the Bible is the living word of God.[49]

Furthermore, Heschel played a major role in shaping the Church's view of Judaism. He was the most important Jewish voice during the meeting of the Second Vatican Council (1962–1965). Heschel spent a great deal of time with Augustine Cardinal Bea, S.J., who, at that time, headed the Secretariat for Promoting Christian Unity and was responsible for drafting the Church's revolutionary renunciation of anti-Semitism in *Nostra Aetate*. Heschel even convinced Pope Paul VI to remove an offensive paragraph that (against Cardinal Bea's wishes) called for Jews to convert to Christianity. After this document came out, Heschel said that what was of the greatest significance for him was "the omission of any reference to the conversion of the Jews."⁵⁰

Heschel was beloved by Christians, especially by Catholics, for his profound religious thought and for the inspiring way he lived. But what did Heschel think of Christianity, or, for that matter, of other traditions? Did he feel that Judaism was the only true religion? Did he feel that all religions are equally valid? How did this committed Jewish thinker grapple with the question of religious diversity?

Many Christian theologians consider religious diversity to be one of the most important issues of our time. It is now nearly fifty years since the distinguished Christian theologian and historian of religion, Wilfred Cantwell Smith, said this about religious diversity:

"This is really as big an issue, almost, as the question of how one accounts theologically for evil—but Christian theologians have been much more conscious of the fact of evil than that of religious pluralism."⁵¹

Since that time, numerous Christian theologians have struggled to arrive at a Christian theology of religions that would be consistent with the new awareness of religious diversity.

The Exclusivist View

Several prominent Christian theologians who have contemplated the issue of religious diversity speak of three major models: exclusivist, inclusivist, and pluralist.⁵² Traditionally, Christians, like believers of many other faiths, have seen Christianity as the only true path to salvation and all other paths as false. This is the exclusivist view.

The Inclusivist View

The inclusivist view is more accepting of other religions. According to this approach, the grace of Christ is present in other traditions; therefore, members of other religions may attain salvation. The inclusivist view, which had advocates in the early Church, was developed in great detail by the eminent Jesuit theologian Karl Rahner (1904–1984), who was very influential in the Second Vatican Council. He held that the Christian tradition is "the absolute religion, intended for all men…"[53] However, since God desires to save all human beings, "there are supernatural, grace-filled elements in non-Christian religions."[54] Pope John Paul II, the world's most famous inclusivist, stated, "Respect and esteem for the other and for what he has in the depths of his heart are essential to dialogue."[55]

The Pluralist View

Pluralism takes an even more expansive view of other religions. The prominent Catholic theologian, Paul Knitter, has presented the pluralist perspective in a most perceptive and persuasive way:

> Other religions may be just as effective and successful in bringing their followers to truth, and peace and well-being with God as Christianity has been for Christians—Only if Christians are truly open to the possibility—that there are many true, saving religions and that Christianity is one among the ways in which God has touched and transformed our world—only then can authentic dialogue take place."[56]

John Hick, the best-known exponent of the pluralist position, explains that for the pluralist, it is fundamental that one does not elevate one's own religion "as uniquely superior to all the others."[57] This means, among other things, that when we come to metaphysical claims about God, we cannot consider a vision of a personal God as superior to an impersonal one. We cannot say that mysticism of personality is superior to mysticism of infinity or that theistic mysticism is superior to monistic mysticism. With regard to sacred texts, the religious pluralist will say that he or she is committed to following the Torah or the Vedas or the Qur'an or the New Testament not because that sacred text is superior to other sacred texts but because it is the sacred text of his or her religious tradition.

Generally, Jewish thinkers have not given the same level of attention to religious diversity as have Christian theologians. Heschel remains the most significant Jewish thinker to address this critical issue. In his essay, "No Religion is an Island," Heschel goes so far as to say that no religion has a monopoly on truth or holiness: "In this Aeon diversity of religions is the will of God."[58] This statement is certainly open to different interpretations. I believe that it means that Heschel accepted the validity of other religious traditions. By saying that religions are the will of God, I believe he means there is also a divine element in these traditions. Heschel cites a Talmudic source that clearly supports this interpretation: "It is a well-established tradition in Jewish literature that the Lord sent prophets to the nations, and even addressed Himself directly to them."[59] According to Heschel, "The Jews do not maintain that the way of the Torah is the only way of serving God."[60]

The Jewish tradition has long regarded the righteous of all nations as having a share in the world to come. Heschel goes further, stating that no religion has a monopoly on truth or holiness. He wrote: "I call heaven and earth to witness that the Holy Spirit rests upon each person, Jew or Gentile, man or woman, master or slave, in consonance with his deeds."[61] For Heschel, it is less important what religious path people follow than that they show compassion for their fellow human beings. In his view, "Religion is a means, not an end."[62] He says: "The prophets convey to us the certainty that human life is sacred, that the most important thing a person can do is to have compassion for his fellow man."[63] The end of religion is to ennoble, to refine, to transform us so that we really have concern for others—which makes us truly human. This teaching is in keeping with his idea that God's outstanding characteristic is "divine pathos." In Heschel's mind, the ultimate goal of human life is to care about humanity as much as God does. This vision enables him to see the saintliness in many of the Christians whom he encountered.

Heschel stresses that "diversity of religions is the will of God" and that "the Jews do not maintain that the way of the Torah is the only way of serving God." Should we then see him as a Jewish pluralist? While Heschel sees all religions as valid, he does not see them as fundamentally equal. A study of Heschel's works reveals that he was quite familiar with some of the primary sources of Christianity and Islam as well as those of Hinduism and Buddhism. In his interpretation of these sources, he stresses the unique aspects of each religion, its distinctiveness, and particularity. He is critical of certain aspects of Asian thought as well as of certain doctrines of Judaism and Christianity. His critique of other religions suggests that Heschel differs from pluralists like Hick, who says it is fundamental that one not elevate one's own religion. While Heschel does not hold that

Judaism is the only true religion and agrees with Knitter and Hick that all religious traditions produce saints, he does not see all traditions as equal. They are all valid, but they are not *equally* valid.

For Heschel, the most fundamental concept of Biblical thought is that God is in search of human beings, that God is a God of pathos who needs human beings and is affected by their actions. Heschel's entire theological structure rests on the assumption that there is a personal God, a God who makes demands on human beings and is concerned and involved with us. Heschel has great difficulty with any system of thought that does not involve a personal concept of God.

In *God in Search of Man*, Heschel asserts that the Hebrew Bible is superior to other sacred texts: "The Bible is mankind's greatest privilege. It is so...Categorical in its demands and full of compassion in its understanding of the human situation. No other book so loves and respects the life of man."[64] Heschel then raises the question, "Why does the Bible surpass everything created by man? Why is there no work worthy of comparison with it? Why is there no substitute for the Bible, no parallel to the history it has engendered? Why must all who seek the living God turn to its pages?"[65]

Heschel responds to his own questions thus: "Set the Bible beside any of the truly great books produced by the genius of man, and see how they are diminished in stature... Other books you can estimate, you can measure, compare; the Bible you can only extol. Its insights surpass our standards. There is nothing greater."[66] He concludes that "just as it is impossible to conceive of God without the world, so it is impossible to conceive of His concern without the Bible... If God is alive, then the Bible is His voice. No other work is as worthy of being considered a manifestation of His will."[67]

Heschel's elevation of the Hebrew Bible seems to suggest that he has an inclusivist rather than a pluralist perspective. Christian inclusivists like John Paul II would agree with Heschel when he states that the aim of dialogue is to overcome "hardness of heart" and to cultivate "a sense of wonder and mystery in unlocking doors to holiness in time."[68] But Heschel differs radically from Christian inclusivists in his opposition to conversion and the creation of a monolithic religious society. Heschel's view of the Hebrew Bible as the greatest religious book is not analogous to Pope John Paul II's view that sees Jesus as the only source of God's salvation and that interreligious dialogue is part of the Church's evangelizing mission.

Heschel's view of other faiths, including the aim of dialogue and his opposition to evangelism, is remarkably similar to the view of Tenzin Gyatso, the fourteenth Dalai Lama, one of the most loved and respected religious leaders in the world today, who is seen by Buddhists as a living incarnation of a Buddha. For the Dalai Lama, as for Heschel, the fact that there are different religions is something beautiful that should be celebrated. But that is not to say that all religions are equal.

The Dalai Lama believes that from a Buddhist perspective, one does not attain liberation while still attached to the idea of a permanent self. There is no enduring person, permanent self, or immortal soul, as Jews and Christians claim. For the Dalai Lama, as for many Mahayana Buddhists, the Buddha had different teachings for different people. From this perspective, other great religious teachers and founders of religions may be seen as bodhisattvas who use skillful means to bring to the world a preliminary teaching, such as the concept of a personal savior god. To the question put to him at "the Bodhgaya interviews" – "But is it only the Buddha who can be the ultimate source of refuge?" the Dalai Lama responded:

> Liberation in which "a mind that understands the sphere of reality annihilates all defilements in the sphere of reality" is a state that only Buddhists can accomplish. This kind of *moksa* or nirvana is only explained in the Buddhist scriptures and is achieved only through Buddhist practice. According to certain religions, however, salvation is a place, a beautiful paradise, like a peaceful valley. To attain such a state as this, to achieve such a state of *moksa*, does not require the practice of emptiness, the understanding of reality. [69]

This statement by the Dalai Lama is not consistent with John Hick's view of other faiths. While both the Dalai Lama and Heschel viewed their own traditions as somehow better and are also deeply committed to their own paths, they are opposed to proselytism and make no claim that they have exclusive possession of ultimate truth. I repeat Heschel's statements: "Holiness is not the monopoly of any religion or tradition" and that "the Jews do not maintain that the way of the Torah is the only way of God."

In *Ethics for the New Millennium*, the Dalai Lama writes:

> In my own case, I am convinced that Buddhism provides me with the most effective framework within which to situate my efforts to develop spiritually through cultivating love and

compassion. At the same time, I must acknowledge that while Buddhism represents the best path for me – that is, it suits my character, my temperament, my inclinations, and my cultural background – the same will be true of Christianity for Christians. For them, Christianity is the best way. On the basis of my conviction, I cannot, therefore, say that Buddhism is best for everyone.[70]

In this book, the Dalai Lama's core message is the necessity of love and compassion, which is precisely the message of Heschel: "The greatest heresy is despair of men's power for goodness, men's power for love."[71] In the Jewish tradition, we are commanded to love all human beings because all are created in the image of God. For Heschel, as for the great second-century sage Rabbi Akiva, the supreme principle of the Torah is "Love thy neighbor as thyself."

Heschel was very much in love with the Jewish tradition and the Jewish people, but his greatness lies in his ability to extend this love to everyone, to see the humanity in everyone, and recognize the divinity in all religious traditions. His love and compassion have brought great healing and great hope to all who have encountered him through the example of his life and the eloquence of his written word.

Heschel was an interreligious artist. His unique view of religious diversity is neither that of a pluralist nor an inclusivist. He transcended the categories created by Christian scholars by artfully affirming that no religion has a monopoly on truth or holiness while raising up the Hebrew Bible as "the only book in the whole world that can never be replaced."

Chapter 4
"To Be is to Stand For"

Abraham Joshua Heschel's friendship with Maurice Friedman and Martin Luther King, Jr.

During the three decades that Abraham Joshua Heschel lived in the United States (1940-1972), he formed deep friendships with some of the most eminent clergy and academics of his generation. Heschel was especially close to Reinhold Niebuhr, perhaps the most influential Protestant thinker of the twentieth century. Ursula Niebuhr claims that "for the last twelve years or so of his life, Abraham really was my husband's closest friend."[72] Heschel was also close to the Reverend William Sloan Coffin, the charismatic Protestant preacher, and Daniel Berrigan, the Jesuit priest and poet. Berrigan said that "Heschel was a father to me.... He was a saint."[73] Heschel also developed a deep friendship with Thomas Merton, the most influential American Catholic monk of the twentieth century. In 1996 Merton wrote that Heschel "is the most significant spiritual writer in this country at the moment. I like his depth and his realism. He knows God."[74]

But Heschel's best-known, and perhaps most historically important, friendship was with Martin Luther King, Jr. Heschel believed that King truly represented the spirit of the Hebrew prophets:

> Where in America do we hear a voice like the voice of the prophets of Israel? Martin Luther King is a sign that God has not forsaken the United States of America. God has sent him to us.
>
> His presence is the hope of America. His mission is sacred, his leadership of supreme importance to every one of us.[75]

In turn, Dr. King has a deep appreciation for Heschel. He spoke of Heschel as "one of the persons who is relevant at all times, always standing with prophetic insight to guide us through these difficult days."[76] King viewed Heschel as a messenger of God because Heschel's words, "to think of man in terms of white, black, or yellow is more than an error. It is *an eye disease, a cancer of the soul*,"[77] expressed King's own view of the world.

Indeed, Heschel may have played a major role in influencing King to oppose the Vietnam War.[78] In 1965, Heschel was one of the founders of Clergy and Laity Concerned About Vietnam. Heschel spoke out against the war on January 31, 1967, in Washington, D.C. "At this hour, Vietnam is our most urgent, our most disturbing religious problem, a challenge to the whole nation as well as a challenge to every one of us as individuals. Vietnam is a personal problem. To speak about God and remain silent on Vietnam is blasphemous."[79] Two months after Heschel's speech, on April 4th, 1967, King gave one of his most controversial speeches, "Beyond Vietnam: A Time to Break Silence," at Riverside Church in New York City. Heschel was on the podium with King that day.

After King's tragic assassination, Heschel spoke with Harold Flender about his friend:

Yes, Dr. King was a close friend, I, myself, felt dedicated to his movement and to his ideas. I think he was one of the greatest prophetic spirits we had in this century. He brought great blessing to the world, and it is a great loss to America and to the world—to all of us concerned with the rights of man—that this man was so tragically eliminated from our midst. But he remains a blessing, and he continues to be an inspiration. If there is anything in the world, I could do to advance the appreciation of his ideas in our time, I will certainly be ready to do so, and I am trying to perpetuate the great legacy of this man.[80]

Maurice Friedman is primarily known as the friend of Martin Buber and the foremost authority on his life and thought. But Friedman was also a dear friend and "near disciple" of Heschel for almost thirty years. Like Heschel, Friedman was also my teacher.[81] The last time I met with Heschel, on June 13, 1972, he told me how moved he was by Friedman's manuscript for *Touchstones of Reality*. Heschel described the work to Friedman's editor at Dutton as a, "Deeply moving account of a personal pilgrimage of a highly sensitive and rich soul."

Heschel certainly had a serious influence on Friedman's thinking. In the conclusion to his article, "Abraham Heschel among Contemporary Philosophers," Friedman says:

The evaluations that I have made of Heschel's thoughts, from the standpoint of an American raised in a tradition of liberal Judaism, give no adequate indication of my great intellectual and spiritual indebtedness to him in the course of more than a quarter of a century of personal friendship. To Heschel, I owe my understanding of prayer, kavanah, hasidut, wonder and awe, the Psalms as a part of daily living, the Sabbath as a holiday of joy, and many other things Jewish.[82]

Although I know that Friedman marched with King in New York City on April 16, 1967, to protest the war in Vietnam, I am not certain that they actually met. Yet, he was a great admirer of King. In his article "Martin Luther King: An American Gandhi and a Modern Job," Friedman says that King "like Gandhi proclaimed the inseparability of the religious and social revolution."[83] Friedman was also moved by King's vision of "total interrelatedness"[84] and his declaration that "the fight for civil rights could not be divorced from the demand for peace in Vietnam."[85]

I realize that Friedman, professor emeritus of religious studies, philosophy, and comparative literature at San Diego State University, is not as famous as King or Heschel. His influence is not as widespread, his ideas, not as well-known. But for more than fifty years, Friedman has been a teacher in colleges and universities to thousands of students. This has been his primary means to create a more peaceful, loving community.

In his classes as a university professor, Friedman stressed critical thinking, the training of the rational mind. But he did not neglect the spiritual dimension of life. He aimed to establish an I-Thou relationship with his students. For Friedman, the major challenge of the third millennium was "restoring relational trust." Friedman's vision of education was shared by Heschel and certainly by King, who, in his speech to students and faculty at Grinnell College, said, "I believe in changing the heart."[86]

But what unites these three men beyond their shared respect for each other? What do they have in common? What links their thought?

First and foremost, they share a desire to bring about a radical spiritual transformation of humanity. The central problem for them is not the survival of religion but the survival of human beings. Heschel states: "What is needed is a spiritual revolution."[87]

In his written work, Heschel aimed to open human beings to a spiritual dimension that would make them more sensitive to transcendence. Heschel wanted to inspire readers of his works to a new way of thinking and acting that would lead them to live a holy life. He hoped that his work would be seen as "a way of developing sensitivity to God and attachment to his presence." Edward Kaplan claims that Heschel, through his writing style, "sought to provoke a complete transformation of consciousness."[88] All three of our writers hoped for a spiritual, nonviolent revolution. In his speeches, King often called for "a revolution in values."

Looking at the role of religion in human history, the trio found that religion has not always been a force for freedom, justice, and peace. Friedman cites the following statement from Martin Buber *"Religion is the Great Enemy of Mankind."*[89] He was, of course, speaking of religion when it encourages hate rather than love when it causes division rather than unity.

Similarly, Heschel stated:

> Religion as an institution, the Temple as an ultimate end, or, in other words, religion for religion's sake, is idolatry. The fact is that evil is integral to religion, not only to secularism. Parochial saintliness may be an evasion of duty and accommodation to selfishness.

> Religion is for God's sake. The human side of religion, its creeds, rituals, and institutions, is a way rather than the goal. The goal is "to do justice, to love mercy, and to walk humbly with God." When the human side of religion becomes the goal, injustice becomes a way.[90]

King was also critical of what he saw as serious distortions of religion. In his sermon "Transformed Nonconformist," speaking on the problem of conformity to the world, he states:

> Nowhere is the tragic tendency to conform more evident than in the church. The mere fact that slavery, racial segregation, war, and economic exploitation have been sanctioned by the church is fit testimony to the fact that the church has more often conformed to the authority of the world than to the authority of God.[91]

Yet, in spite of the evil committed in the name of religion, Heschel, Friedman, and King did not give up on their traditions. They never forsook the idea that religion is the way to heal the world, that religion can be a way to bring about peace. Heschel could have been speaking for his two friends when he said, "What is needed at this very moment is to mobilize all human beings for one great task, to achieve world peace.[92]

All three felt that religious exclusivism was a major threat to the peace of the world. The common belief among pious people that there is only one valid religion can lead to hatred and violence and even war against the other, the stranger, the member of a different religious tradition. At a minimum, it is a great obstacle to authentic interfaith dialogue. All three believed that religions working together could become a force for peace. But unfortunately, in the words of Heschel, "Our terrible sin is not giving peace absolute priority. It is conceivable for states to get together and have a United Nations, but it is still inconceivable to have a United Religions. The situation is very grave."[93] On this point, also King fully agreed with Heschel: "It is not enough to say, 'We must not wage war.' It is necessary to love peace and sacrifice for it. We must concentrate not merely on the eradication of war but on the affirmation of peace."[94] This view is shared by Maurice Friedman:

> The greatest task of contemporary man is not to build 'enlightened' utopias but to build peace in the context in which he finds himself. The true peacemakers are those who take upon themselves, in the most concrete manner conceivable, the task of discovering what can be done in each situation of tension and struggle by way of facing the real conflicts and working toward genuine reconciliation.[95]

In his essay "No Religion is An Island," Heschel presents a radical view of the world's religions. He argues that no religion has a monopoly on truth or holiness and says, "In this aeon diversity of religions is the will of God."[96] For Heschel, "Religion is a means, not an end."[97] In a similar vein, Friedman states in *Touchstones of Reality*, one of his most personal books:

The reality of pluralism must be the starting point of any serious modern faith. We should give up looking for the one true religion and consider our religious commitments as unique relationships to a truth that we cannot possess. We should also give up the notion that some men possess the spirit and others do not.[98]

Friedman was well aware of the affinities between his and Heschel's views.[99] In his essay, "Abraham Joshua Heschel and Interreligious Dialogue," Friedman says:

> On rereading Heschel's essay "No Religion is an Island," I am astonished at how fully what Heschel says about interreligious cooperation corresponds to my own approach to interreligious dialogue via what I call the 'dialogue of touchstones.' In the Human way, I claim that the only realistic modern approach is that of religious pluralism. This is exactly what Heschel says and in the same spirit of dialogue and even of a dialogue of touchstones.[100]

In this essay, Friedman cites numerous passages from Heschel's article, including:

> Holiness is not the monopoly of any particular religion or tradition. Wherever a deed is done in accord with the will of God, wherever a thought of man is directed toward Him, there is the holy.[101]

What then is the purpose of interreligious cooperation? ... [It is] to cooperate in trying to bring about a resurrection of sensitivity, a revival of conscience; to keep alive the divine sparks in our souls, to nurture openness to the spirit of the Psalms, reverence for the words of the prophets, and faithfulness to the Living God.[102]

In a letter to me on July 17, 1986, accompanying his manuscript on Heschel, Friedman says: "I think no reader can doubt what I say: that we are in astonishing agreement and that what I write is very much in his spirit."

Based on my study of King, he fully supports Heschel's and Friedman's view of other religions. In his 1953 sermon 'Communism's Challenge to Christianity,' King said, "Historic world religions such as Judaism, Mohammedanism, Buddhism, Hinduism may be listed as possible alternatives to Christianity..."[103] In *To Make the Wounded Whole: The Cultural Legacy of Martin Luther King, Jr.*, Lewis Baldwin writes that "King held that the personal relationship with God, when examined from the standpoint of the Christian faith, encouraged religious tolerance and respect for religious pluralism.[104]

For King, Friedman, and Heschel, no religion has a monopoly on God. God is found in human hearts everywhere, not just in one religious' tradition. What is most significant is how an individual acts in his or her everyday life to enhance the power of human love, peace, and justice. As men who united life of prayer with a life of action, they lived their ideal of interreligious dialogue. Heschel and King were involved mainly with Jews and Christians, while Friedman was deeply committed to dialogue with members of all the major world religions.[105] In his "Letter from Birmingham Jail," which he addressed to Jewish, Catholic, and Protestant clergy, King said: "Too long has our beloved Southland been bogged down in a tragic effort to live in monologue rather than dialogue."[106] A study of King reveals that he was influenced by Martin Buber's vision of dialogue, especially the distinction that Buber made between the "I-It" relationship and the "I-Thou" relationship. With these two interactions in mind, King said, "Segregation, to use the terminology of the Jewish philosopher Martin Buber, substitutes an 'I-It' relationship for an 'I-Thou' relationship and ends up relegating persons to the status of things. Hence segregation is not only politically, economically, and sociologically unsound, it is morally wrong and sinful."[107]

These three great men clearly had similar views on the potential for the corruption of religion, religious pluralism, and the need for interfaith dialogue, but is there a common inspiration for their views? Martin Buber is perhaps the greatest single influence on Friedman, and there can be no doubt that Jesus was the major influence on King. But when we compare the talks that King and Heschel each gave at the same conference in 1963, we see that the major theological link between them is reverence for the Hebrew Bible, especially the prophets.[108]

Heschel and King first met at the National Conference on Religion and Race in Chicago in 1963. At this conference, Heschel, "a brand plucked from the fire," who had experienced Nazi racism firsthand, presented one of the most powerful speeches of his life.[109] In his talk, "The Religious Basis of Equality of Opportunity—The Segregation of God," Heschel said that "racism is worse than idolatry. Racism is Satanism, unmitigated evil. The aim of this conference is first of all to state clearly the stark alternative. I call heaven and earth to witness against you this day: I have set before you religion and race, life and death, blessing and curse. Choose life."[110] Heschel, who had just recently completed his major work *The Prophets* (1962), said: "All prophecy is one great exclamation; God is not indifferent to evil! He is always concerned. He is personally affected by what man does to man. He is a God of pathos."[111] To bring about change, Heschel said: "What we need is a total mobilization of heart, intelligence, and wealth for the purpose of love and justice. God is in search of men, waiting, hoping for man to do His will.[112] Although Heschel often stated that the "humanity of man is no longer self-evident,"[113] he insisted that there is always hope: "The greatest heresy is despair, despair of men's power for goodness, men's power for love."[114]

In this talk, Heschel also presented his concept of the human being, which he believed to be the core of Judaism. For Heschel, the fundamental statement about human beings in the Hebrew Bible is that human beings are created in God's image: "God is every man's pedigree. He is either the Father of all men or of no man. The image of God is either in every man or in no man."[115] Heschel ended his talk at Chicago with the following word of the Prophet Amos (5:24): "Let justice roll down like waters and righteousness like a mighty stream."

Heschel's stress on the sacred image of the human, which he believed was the central issue in religious education, is also emphasized in King's speech: "Deeply rooted in our religious heritage is the conviction that every man is an heir to a legacy of dignity and worth. Our Judeo-Christian tradition refers to this inherent dignity of man in the Biblical term the *image of God*."[116] This Biblical idea, which was central to our three thinkers, is, in my view, one of the main motivating forces for their involvement in social action.

Amazingly, toward the end of his speech, King also cites the cry of Amos: "Let justice roll down like waters and righteousness like an ever-flowing stream."[117] This is significant. It was Amos who declared that the people of Israel were not more precious to God than the Egyptians, the Philistines, or the Syrians (Amos 9:7). The voice that the Prophet Amos hears tells him that God wants to liberate everyone, not just Jews. Friedman, Heschel, and King looked to the prophets as their models, and therefore they too spoke and acted for the liberation of all people, especially the poor and the oppressed.

In her article "Theological Affinities in the Writings of Abraham Joshua Heschel and Martin Luther King, Jr." Susannah Heschel says:

> A Comparison of King and Heschel reveals theological affinities in addition to shared political sympathies. Heschel's concept of divine pathos, a category central to his theology, is mirrored in King's understanding of the nature of God's involvement with humanity. For both, the theological was intimately intertwined with the political, and that conviction provided the basis of the spiritual affinity they felt for each other.[118]

Her following statement captures the most important affinity between Heschel and King: "[M]ost striking is the commonality between the spirituality taught by Heschel and King, rooted in the emphasis King gave to the Hebrew Bible and the Exodus narrative and in Heschel's emphasis on the prophets."[119]

Barely five months before his death, King delivered a speech titled "Remaining Awake During a Revolution" at Grinnell College in Iowa, the college at which I have been teaching since 1972. During this historic event for our college, King spoke about his love for all human beings and his concern for the survival of humanity. He stressed the fact that all of life is interrelated and that we must end racial injustice. He repeated the cry of Amos, "Let justice roll down like waters and righteousness like a mighty stream." His core message was that before Amos's statement could become a reality, we must realize that "No man is an island, entire of itself." We must talk to each other and be fully present to each other. As King put it: "[To] stand-alone or live alone in the world today is sleeping through a revolution." King, Heschel, and Friedman were fully awake during the revolution.

Chapter 5

Swami Vivekananda and Rabbi Abraham Joshua Heschel: Saving the World

> My thesis, therefore, is no world peace without peace among religions, no peace among religions without dialogue between the religions, and no dialogue between the religions without accurate knowledge of one another.[120]

Clergy, he insists, must see beyond the beauty and enrichment religion has brought to millions of believers and recognize the violence, suffering, and destruction too often committed in the name of theological exclusivity and claims to infallibility.

The main obstacle to authentic interfaith dialogue is the belief that truth is the domain of one religious tradition exclusively. I have drawn inspiration from two visionary spiritual leaders—a swami and a rabbi—who embrace religious diversity while being deeply committed to their own faiths. I am referring to Swami Vivekananda (1863–1902) and Rabbi Abraham Joshua Heschel (1907–1972).

Though Swami Vivekananda was a Hindu monist and Heschel a Jewish theist, their views on many significant issues, such as their views of other religious traditions, their concept of humanity, and their vision of God, were remarkably similar. By similar, I do not mean identical; their differences are real. However, in the sphere of interfaith understanding, their points of agreement outweigh their difference. Familiarity with the philosophies of these two thinkers invites an appreciation of the spirituality of all people of faith.

Both Vivekananda and Heschel were critical of certain aspects and doctrines of their own traditions. Their concern was not on theological subtleties but rather on the righteousness of each human being. Both believed that for an individual to attain this goal, one must attempt to experience God in one's own life to truly come to feel the presence of God.

Vivekananda believed that the mystical feeling of being in God's presence is preceded by ethical discipline: "He reveals Himself to the pure heart; the pure and the stainless see God, yea, even in this life. Then all doubt ceases. So, the best proof a Hindu sage gives about God is: "I have seen God."[121]

Similarly, Abraham Joshua Heschel, one of the authentic Jewish mystics of the twentieth century, cites the Hebrew Bible as a source of Jewish longing for immediate contact with the Divine: "Not all of the people of the Bible are satisfied with awareness of God's power and presence. There are those 'that seek Him, that seek Thy face O God of Jacob' (Psalms 24:6) ... At Sinai, according to legend, Israel was not content to receive the divine words through an intermediary. They said to Moses, "We want to hear the words of our King from Himself... We want to see our King."[122] Heschel then quotes Judah Halevi, the great medieval Jewish poet: "To see the face of my King is my sole desire. I fear none but Him; I revere only Him. Would that I might see Him in a dream! I would continue to sleep for all eternity. Would that I might behold His face within my heart! Mine eyes would never ask to look at anything else."[123] Throughout his works, Heschel speaks of the Divine-human encounter, of the possibility of experiencing the presence of God.

Heschel and Vivekananda would agree that to achieve spiritual transformation, one must "forget the self," setting the stage for experiencing a tremendous concern for other human beings and the world. For them, saving the world seems to be more central than personal salvation. In fact, personal salvation is undertaken only as a means of saving the world. Throughout his writings, Vivekananda emphasizes the divine nature of human beings. According to him, the central aim of man and woman lies in "aiding humanity to realize its own true, divine nature."[124]

This emphasis is also found in the thought of Heschel. He insists that the fundamental statement about human beings, according to the Jewish tradition, is found in the following passage in Genesis: "And God said, 'I will make man in My image, after My likeness...' And God created man in His image, in the image of God He created him; male and female He created them" (Gen 1:26–27). Heschel interprets this statement as follows:

> The intention is not to identify, "the image and likeness," with a particular quality or attribute of man, such as reason, speech, power, or skill. It does not refer to something which in later systems was called "the best in man," "the divine spark," "the eternal spirit," or "the immortal element" in man. It is the whole man and every man who was made in the image and likeness of God. It is both

body and soul, sage and fool, saint and sinner, man in his joy and in his grief, in his righteousness and wickedness. The image is not in man; it is man.[125]

Vivekananda and Heschel agree that religion cannot be separated from social and political issues. In order to bring about the kingdom of God on earth and beautify all parts of our globe, love of God must manifest itself in love and compassion for all human beings. Vivekananda teaches that "the gist of all worship [is] to be good and to do good to others"[126] and that "each is responsible for the evil anywhere in the world."[127] Similarly, Heschel teaches that "only a free person knows that the true meaning of existence is experienced in giving, in endowing, in meeting a person face to face, in fulfilling other people's needs"[128] and that "some are guilty, all are responsible."[129] Here is where their affinity is strongest.

At the World Parliament of Religions on September 11, 1893, Vivekananda made two memorable statements on religious tolerance:

> I am proud to belong to a religion that has taught the world both tolerance and universal acceptance. We not only believe in universal toleration, but we accept all religions as true.[130]

> If the Parliament of Religions has shown anything to the world, it is this: It has proved to the world that holiness, purity, and charity are not the exclusive possessions of any church in the world and that every system has produced men and women of the most exalted character."[131]

Heschel believed that dialogue "between the River Jordan and the River Ganges" would enrich Judaism and that it was "vitally important... for Judaism to reach out into non-Jewish culture in order to absorb elements which it may use for the enrichment of its life and thought."[132]

In his inaugural address delivered at Union Theological Seminary in 1965, Heschel presented a view of the religions of the world that is fully in the spirit of tolerance expressed by Vivekananda at the World Parliament of Religions. Heschel asserted: "Perhaps it is the will of God that in this aeon there should be diversity in our forms of devotion and commitment to Him. In this aeon, diversity of religions is the will of God."[133] Here Heschel seems to leave little doubt that Jews, Christians, and Muslims, in their various ways, are truly worshipping God. But would this statement apply to other world religions whose concept of God is totally different from that of the Jewish tradition? Heschel quotes a passage from the Prophet Malachi and follows it with an interpretation that indicates that Eastern traditions are also valid to him:

> From the rising of the sun to its setting, My name is great among the nations, and in every place, incense is offered to My name, and a pure offering; for My name is great among the nations, says the Lord of Hosts (Malachi 1:11).

This statement refers undoubtedly to the contemporaries of the prophet. But who were these worshippers of One God? At the time of Malachi, there were few proselytes. Yet the statement declares: "All those who worship their gods do not know it, but they are really worshipping Me. It seems that the prophet proclaims that men all over the world, though they confess different conceptions of God, are really worshipping One God, the Father of all men, though they may not be aware of it."[134]

It appears to me that Heschel's understanding of Malachi comes very close to the spirit of Vivekananda, exemplified in the following statement made by his guru Sri Ramakrishna: "Supposing it is a mistake to worship God in the image—doesn't he know he alone is being worshipped? He will certainly be pleased by that worship."[135]

Heschel's interpretation of the Hebrew Bible and his belief that religious pluralism is the will of God not only has created a rich atmosphere for Jewish-Christian dialogue but also has opened the door to Jewish encounters with Eastern traditions.

Since Heschel's death in 1972, his pluralistic perspective on other faiths has found support among outstanding Jewish thinkers, including a few seminal Orthodox rabbis of our time. Rabbi Irving Greenberg stated: "Any claim that one understanding of God is the definitive, superior one is a form of idolatry."[136] He goes on to say, "God, too, has many messengers. Pluralism leads me to recognize that the overflowing love of the Divine is never exhausted. My presence, my mind, my revelation, no matter how great, cannot exhaust infinity."[137] Rabbi David Hartman found that a critical task for Jewish thinkers today is to show that one can be a passionate, committed Jew without holding that Judaism is the only true religion:

> We must aspire to develop religious forms of commitment and passion that do not require believing that only one tradition reflects the truth. The vitality of religious commitment is not necessarily a function of exclusivity and uniqueness. The presence of other religious

traditions need not threaten a person's total devotion and commitment to a particular tradition. Affirmation does not entail the delegitimization of "the other."[138]

In *The Dignity of Difference: Avoiding the Clash of Civilizations*, Jonathan Sacks, the former chief rabbi of Britain and the Commonwealth, makes a most profound case for a pluralistic view. Written as a response to the tragic events of September 11, 2001, the book reflects on the power of religion as a force for good and evil. Sacks believes that "men kill because they believe they possess the truth while their opponents are in error." For Sacks, as for Greenberg and Hartman, "Truth on earth is not, nor can it aspire to be, the whole truth... In heaven, there is truth; on earth, there are truths."[21] In the spirit of Heschel and in almost identical words, Sacks writes: "that the truth at the beating heart of monotheism is that God is greater than religion; that He is only partially comprehended by any faith."[139]

For Vivekananda and Heschel, what religious path an individual follows is less important than living a pious and humane life. They believed that an encounter with God makes one more human and enhances the ethical quality of one's life.

Placing the thinking of Vivekananda and Heschel side by side not only helped me to understand the spirit of tolerance in the Hindu tradition; it helped me to see that the spirit of tolerance is very much alive in Jewish tradition.

Chapter 6

Pope John Paul II: A Jewish Perspective on a Polish Catholic Saint

> As Christians and Jews, following the example of the faith of Abraham, we are called to be a blessing for the world... This is the common task awaiting us. It is, therefore, necessary for us, Christians, and Jews, to first be a blessing to one another.
>
> John Paul II, April 6, 1993[140]

No person has done more to heal the rift between Jews and Christians in the 2,000-year history of the Church than Karol Wojtyla, the archbishop of Krakow. I celebrate the sainthood of John Paul II, as well as that of John XXIII, who said, "I want to throw open the windows of the church so that we can see out and the people can see in"[141] and who called the Second Vatican Council, which issued the magnificent document, *Nostra Aetate*. For me, its most significant statement about the acceptance of other religions:

> The Catholic Church rejects nothing that is true and holy in these religions. She regards with sincere reverence those ways of conduct and of life, those precepts, and teachings which, though

differing in many aspects from the ones she holds and sets forth, nonetheless often reflect a ray of that Truth which enlightens all men. (*Nostra Aetate*, no. 2)[142]

Then follows this extraordinary statement:

The Church, therefore, exhorts her sons, that through dialogue and collaboration with the followers of other religions, carried out with prudence and love and in witness to the Christian faith and life, they recognize, preserve, and promote the good things, spiritual and moral, as well as the socio-cultural values found among these men. (Nostra Aetate, no. 2)

For the first time in 2,000 years, the Church rejected the accusation that Jews were collectively to blame for the crucifixion of Jesus. The document clearly states that "God holds the Jews most dear" (*Nostra Aetate*, no. 4). It also deplores antisemitism and affirms that Jesus Christ was born of a young Jewish girl of Nazareth, the Virgin Mary and that most of the early disciples who proclaimed Christ to the world were Jews.

No one devoted more time and energy to making *Nostra Aetate* a reality than John Paul II. I agree with the statement of Cardinal Stanislaw Dziwisz: "You could say that John Paul II's entire pontificate was a continual implementation of Vatican II."[143]

Karol Wojtyla was born May 18, 1920, in Wadowice, Poland, in a house owned by a Jewish family. The Jews of this small town constituted about twenty percent of the population, making John Paul II the first pope since Peter to have grown up among Jews and to have spoken Yiddish.

Jews of Wadowice who knew him to tell us that, even as a young man, he protected Jews from anti-Semites. During World War II, Wojtyla was a member of an underground theater group that worked against the Nazis. When he became pope, he granted his first official audience to one of his oldest friends, Jerzy Kluger, a Jew with whom he grew up in Wadowice.[144]

During John Paul II's twenty-six years as pope, despite some serious disagreements with the Vatican, Jews witnessed the pope's deep veneration and a special love for the Jewish people. This love had a theological as well as a personal basis. The Jews were precious to him because, in his words, they continued to show the world "the beauty and profound truth of belief in the one God and Lord." For the pope, as well as for the Jews, the Hebrew Bible is *Torah min ha-shamayim* (Torah from heaven), coming into being by way of revelation. The God of the Jewish people is the God of the Catholic Church.

I see agreement between Pope John Paul II and Rabbi Abraham Joshua Heschel on the affinity of Jews and Christians. Heschel writes:

> Above all, while dogmas and forms of worship are divergent, God is the same. What unites us? A commitment to the Hebrew Bible as Holy Scripture. Faith in the Creator, the God of Abraham, commitment to many of His commandments, justice, and mercy, a sense of contrition, sensitivity to the sanctity of life and to the involvement of God in history, the conviction that without the holy the good will be defeated, prayer that history may not end before the end of days, and so much more.[145]

Both Heschel and John Paul II aimed to open human beings to a spiritual dimension that would make them more sensitive to transcendence and to inspire people to a way of thinking and acting that would lead them to live a holy life. The most striking affinity between Heschel and the pope is Heschel's assertion, which he repeated again and again that God is in search of human beings. George Weigel, John Paul II's biographer, claimed that for the pope, "the human story is not the story of man's search for God, but rather the story of God's search for us."[146]

One of the keyways in which John Paul II advanced Jewish-Catholic understanding was that, more than any other pope, he renounced the teaching of contempt for Jews. For him, Jews were not rejected by God. He said, "God does not reject his people."[147] He spoke of antisemitism as "'a sin against God and humanity.'"[148] For the pope, there was only one race: the human race. He suported the assertion in the 1974 *Vatican Guidelines* that Christians should strive to understand Jews as they "define themselves in the light of their own religious experience."[149]

Another factor in John Paul II's effectiveness in improving relations with Judaism was his frequent acknowledgment that the Jews were the primary victims of the Holocaust. He did not deny or downplay the horror of the Holocaust. He visited Auschwitz in 1979 and spoke of what happened in that place as "one of the darkest and most tragic moments in history,"[150] and also as "the greatest tragedy of our century: the greatest trauma.'"[151] Other indications of the pope's understanding of and sensitivity to the Holocaust were his hosting of a concert in memory of the victims and his intervention to resolve the crisis caused by the placement of a convent at Auschwitz.

Another way in which he built bridges with Judaism was through formal recognition of the State of Israel. In 1994 the Vatican established full diplomatic relations. Symbolic of this new relationship was the menorah-lighting at the Vatican to mark Israel's fifty years of statehood.

On April 13, 1986, Pope John Paul II went inside the synagogue of Rome and blessed the Jews, which he singled out as the major event of that year.[152] He believed that this event would be remembered "for centuries and millennia in the history of this city and this church. I thank Divine Providence because the task was given to me."[153] It was during this visit that the pope made the following extraordinary statement on the strong bond that united the Catholic Church with the Jewish people, which he based on *Nostra Aetate*:

> The Church of Christ discovers her "bond" with Judaism by "searching into her own mystery" (NA 4). The Jewish religion is not "extrinsic" to us, but in a certain way, is "intrinsic" to our own religion. With Judaism, therefore, we have a relationship that we do not have with any other religion. You are our dearly beloved brothers and, in a certain way, it could be said that you are our elder brothers.[154]

Perhaps the most significant interfaith event of the John Paul II papacy was his Jubilee Pilgrimage to Israel in March of 2000. One of the primary reasons for the pope's visit to the Holy Land was to walk where Jesus walked, to be in the places connected with the life, death, and resurrection of Jesus. But, John Paul II, whose passion for peace was unsurpassed, had other major goals for the journey. He hoped to create greater harmony among the various

Christian churches and to promote a dialogue among Jews, Christians, and Muslims in the region. The pope often stated that such dialogue was a priority. On February 24, 2000, John Paul said in Egypt, "To do harm, to promote violence and conflict in the name of religion is a terrible contradiction and a great offense against God."[155]

For Jews throughout the world, perhaps the most emotional moment of the pope's visit to Israel occurred on Thursday, March 23, 2000, when he attended a special ceremony at the Hall of Remembrance at Yad Vashem, Israel's national Holocaust memorial, and stated:

> I have come to Yad Vashem to pay homage to the millions of Jewish people who, stripped of everything, especially of human dignity, were murdered in the Holocaust. More than half a century has passed, but the memories remain... We wish to remember. But we wish to remember for a purpose, namely, to ensure that never again will evil prevail, as it did for the millions of innocent victims of Nazism.[156]

Jews around the world who watched this ceremony on TV recognized that they had just witnessed one of the most extraordinary events in all Jewish history. Rabbi Ronald Kronish, the director of the Interreligious Coordinating Council in Israel, said of this event: "It was the Pope's indomitable spirit on that day—and throughout the trip—that moved Jewish people in Israel and all over the world to tears. It was his spiritual presence that moved Prime Minister [Ehud] Barak to react so positively to his speech." [157] The prime minister began his speech by welcoming the pope to Jerusalem in the name of all the citizens of Israel—Christians, Muslims, Druze, and Jews. Barak continued:

You have done more than anyone else to bring about the historical change in the attitude of the Church towards the Jewish people, initiated by the good Pope John the XXIII... And I think I can say, Your Holiness, your coming here today, to the Tent of Remembrance at Yad Vashem is a climax of this historic journey of healing. Here, right now, time itself has come to a standstill... This very moment holds within it two thousand years of history.[158]

For many Jews around the world, the milestone of the pope's pilgrimage took place on Sunday, March 26, his last day in the Holy Land, when he went to the Western Wall in Jerusalem, the holiest place on earth for Jews, and inserted the following prayer into the cracks of the Wall:

God of our fathers,

you chose Abraham and his descendants

to bring your Name to the Nations:

we are deeply saddened by the behaviour of those

who in the course of history

have caused these children of yours to suffer,

and asking your forgiveness, we wish to commit ourselves

to genuine brotherhood

with the people of the Covenant.[159]

The prominent Israeli writer, Amos Oz, spoke of the pope's visit to Israel as "an epochal turning point, a revolution of great historical consequence."[160] Rabbi David

Rosen, director of the Anti-Defamation League's Israel office, said, "We deeply appreciate the Pope's historic contribution to Christian contrition for past attitudes towards the Jewish people that made the soil fertile for the Shoah, and for his profound commitment to Catholic-Jewish reconciliation."[161]

In a joint statement, the Central Conference of American Rabbis and the Rabbinical Assembly, representing 3,000 Reform and Conservative rabbis, expressed deep gratitude and praise for the pope's contribution to Christian-Jewish relations. The last paragraph reads:

> Borrowing from the Pope's terminology, we call upon our rabbinic constituents to engage in intensified dialogue and fellowship with our Roman Catholic neighbors. At this historic moment of the first papal pilgrimage to the sovereign Jewish State, may the inspiring leadership of Pope John Paul II lead us toward greater reconciliation, friendship, and partnership in effecting *tikkun olam* ["healing the world"].[162]

I agree with George Weigel, who wrote in his biography of John Paul II that because of his pontificate, "Catholics and Jews stand on the edge of a new theological conversation."[163]

Not only will John Paul II be remembered for his remarkable contribution to Jewish-Christian relations, but also for his deep devotion to interfaith dialogue with members of other world religions. He saw interfaith dialogue as a way to lead us to realize that we are all God's children. In this spirit, he convened one of the most remarkable interfaith events in history, the World Day of

Prayer for Peace, held at Assisi in 1986. Leaders from all the world's major religions participated, and at the conclusion, John Paul II spoke of a common goal "to seek the truth, to love and serve all individuals and peoples, and therefore to make peace among individuals and among nations."[164]

The greatness of John Paul II was his ability to extend his love to all Catholics and all of humanity. He will be remembered as a defender of the Jewish people, as a saint for Shalom.

Chapter 7
Three Modern Muslim Perceptions of Judaism and Christianity

In present times, when many perceive Islam to be perpetually hostile toward other religious traditions, it is important to remember that there is a spectrum of opinions in the field of Muslim theology. Like other religious traditions, Islam has its exclusivists, its inclusivists, and its pluralists. Chief among the modern exclusivists is Sayyid Abul A'la Mawdudi (1903–1979), who is probably the single most widely-read writer among Muslims. For Mawdudi, Islam is the only authentic God-ordained path to salvation.

Isma'il Raji al Faruqi (1921–1986), a former professor of Islamic studies at Temple University, is an inclusivist, who says that Christians and Jews—fellow "People of the Book"—can be saved if they believe in God and the Day of Judgment and live ethical lives.

Seyyed Hossein Nasr (b. 1933), one of the most brilliant Muslim scholars currently teaching in the United States, is a pluralist who says: "To have lived any religion fully is to have lived all religions..."[165]

All three are orthodox Muslims, though present radically different attitudes toward other religious traditions. They share the belief that the Qur'an is the Word of God and that Muhammad received the Qur'an verbatim from heaven. They all reject as heretical the notion of a human element in the Qur'an. Nasr writes: "I know of no Muslim, not even one who no longer lives within the Islamic world (*dar al-islam*), whose writings are accepted in any Islamic country, who has not asserted that the Qur'an is the Word of God."[166]

Sayyid Abul A'la Mawdudi

Mawdudi believed that most Muslims do not really understand Islam and that very few of them practice it wholeheartedly. He was convinced that if Muslims truly practiced Islam, the entire world would convert. According to Mawdudi, only the Muslim may attain salvation, which requires accepting the Qur'an as the final true revelation from God and Muhammad as His final prophet. If you reject Muhammad, you are a *kaffir* or infidel.

Mawdudi claimed that no unbiased person who studies the life and teaching of Muhammad can escape the conclusion that Muhammad was a true prophet of God and that the Qur'an is the "true Book of God." While Mawdudi conceded that there had been other authentic prophets, including Jesus and Moses, he believed that their followers distorted their teachings, making it impossible to know what in Christian and Jewish scripture derives from God and what from humans: "The original and the fictitious, the Divine and the human are so intermingled that the grain cannot be separated from the chaff... The Qur'an, on the other hand, is fully preserved and not a jot or tittle has been changed or left out of it."[167]

Mawdudi argued that all the true prophets were really Muslims: "Although the religion taught by Jesus Christ (peace be upon him) was none but *Islam*, his followers reduced it into a hodgepodge called Christianity..."[168]

Isma'il Raji al Faruqi

Isma'il Raji al Faruqi was one of the most prominent Muslim scholars actively engaged in dialogue with Christians and Jews. He represented Islam at significant national and international interfaith conferences, of which he was a driving and organizing force. Al Faruqi claimed that in the West, Islam is the most unknown, most misunderstood, and most demeaned religious tradition, not only by the population in general but also by some influential historians of religion:

> It is the only religion that contended and fought with most of the world religions on their own home ground, whether in the field of ideas or on the battlefields of history... Moreover, Islam is the only religion that in its interreligious and international conflict with Judaism, Christianity, Hinduism, and Buddhism, succeeded significantly and in major scale in all the fights it undertook... No wonder, then, that it is the religion with the greatest number of enemies and, hence, the religion most misunderstood.[169]

Al Faruqi claimed that the distortion of Islam is also due to a number of influential twentieth-century Christian writers whose works contributed to a negative vision of Islam. He admitted, however, that Muslims sometimes distort the truth. In his book *Christian Ethics*, he argued that not everything in Sufism is in accord with the teachings of Islam: "That which had developed into the Sufi movement of history contained something utterly un-Islamic cannot be doubted." For al Faruqi, the only certain truth is the Qur'an, which for him is "the work of God in His own words."[170]

Well aware that adherents of many other religious traditions also claim their tradition is in sole possession of the truth, Al Faruqi addressed the issue of conflicting truth claims. He argued that the Muslim is in the best position to resolve this question because only Islam honors the major religious traditions of the world, especially Judaism and Christianity, with its acknowledgment that initially, they were authentic revelations from God. According to Islam, there have been 124,000 authentic prophets sent to the world, including Moses, Jesus, and perhaps even the Buddha. Like Mawdudi, he asserted that followers falsified the original messages of their prophets, and that's why we have Judaism, Christianity, Buddhism, and so forth. Al Faruqi wrote:

> If all prophets have conveyed one and the same message, whence come all the religions of history? Assuming that they are genuine, Islam answers that there can be no difference in the messages of the prophets since their source is one, namely, God. Revelation through the prophets constitutes a fund of truth for every people because God made His will known to every people in their own language. But Islam asserts that variations of space and time, acculturation by alien influences, and human whims and passions caused people to slip from the truth. The result was that the religions of history all erred more or less from the truth because none has preserved the original text of its revelation. In their pristine

purity, the revelations were one and the same and contained the same principles of religion and ethics. [171]

Where al Faruqi differed markedly from Mawdudi was his attitude towards salvation. Al Faruqi insisted that Christians and Jews who serve God by doing good works need not worry about salvation because "God judges people by their deeds or works, not by rites or ceremonies such as baptism."[172]

For al Faruqi, the ultimate goal of interfaith dialogue is conversion, not understanding: "We must say it boldly that the end of dialogue is conversion; not conversion to my, your, or his religion, culture, mores, or political regime, but to the truth... To win all mankind to the truth is the highest and noblest ideal man has ever entertained." [173] Throughout his writings, al Faruqi stressed that God demands Muslims invite all to the truth; that is, pure, uncorrupted Islam.

Seyyed Hossein Nasr

Seyyed Hossein Nasr, professor of Islamic studies at George Washington University, is one of the outstanding Muslim thinkers involved in interfaith dialogue today. His argument that Islam considers Judaism and Christianity to be authentic religious traditions willed by God is considered radical in many Muslim circles. In his opening statement in *Ideals and Realities of Islam*, perhaps the most widely read book on Islam in the English-speaking world, Nasr writes:

> Every revealed religion is *the* religion and *a* religion, *the* religion in as much as it contains within itself the Truth and means of attaining the Truth, *a* religion since it emphasizes a particular

aspect of the Truth in conformity with the spiritual and psychological needs of the humanity for whom it is destined and to whom it is addressed.[174]

Nasr draws inspiration from the Sufis, the Islamic mystics who he claims have the most profound understanding of divine revelation and are therefore the most qualified to penetrate "the mysterious unity that underlies the diversity of religious forms." [175] Sufis, such as Rumi and ibn Arabi, who were most concerned with the inner meaning of religion, believed in the unity of world religions.

Since the publication of the book, Nasr has continued to stress that "orthodox religions," that is, faiths that have been chosen for human beings by God, all lead to union with God.

Nasr is aware of the conflicting truth claims made by the different religious traditions. He deals with this issue in response to a paper delivered by Hans Küng at Harvard Divinity School in 1984. With regard to the Muslim and Christian visions of Christ, Nasr states: "God in his infinite power and wisdom could create two major world communities holding two different views concerning the earthly end of Christ.[176]

For Nasr, it is certainly possible that God wanted the Muslim community to see Christ differently from the way that the Christian community views Christ. In response to the question, "If Islam says that God was *not* incarnate and Christianity says that God *was* incarnate, could both be true?" Nasr responded:

> I have not worked out all the theological details of this question, but I do not think that it is metaphysically absurd to make such a statement.

> It is nowhere in the Qur'an that the Muslims are forced to refuse to accept what the Christians think of their own "prophet." That is, Islam says that when you look at God as the Absolute, he cannot beget. This does not mean that in another revelation, God has not revealed another aspect of himself. A religion can be based on another aspect of Divinity, and therefore this is not something unworkable."[177]

For Nasr, every authentic revelation is complete in itself, but it does not exhaust the divine nature. Nasr argues, "The Qur'an is the Word of God, but no Muslim ever claimed that it is the *only* word of God." [178]

The exclusivist approach is potentially dangerous because it allows no place for interreligious dialogue or for truth in other religions. It tends to see religious communities as opponents in the battle for human souls. In its extreme form, it can lead to fanaticism, intolerance, and violence.

> The inclusivist and pluralist approaches, on the other hand, allow for dialogue among religious communities. All three Abrahamic traditions, Judaism, Christianity, and Islam, teach of a God who is merciful and just. The prophets of each tradition dream of a world of peace, one in which every person has infinite value. Dialogue, whether it's based on pluralism or inclusivism, helps us realize this vision.

But to dialogue fairly, each religious tradition must take a hard look at its own scriptures and cast a critical eye on those passages that could lead to arrogance, intolerance, or violence.

For Jews, this means reexamining the concept of "the Chosen." For Christians, this means looking critically at the idea that there is no salvation outside the church. For Muslims, it means reexamining the concept of jihad. Muhammad taught that war was the "lesser jihad." The "greater jihad" was the struggle within one's own soul. It is important to remember that all religions have their weaknesses, and all religions have great bounties of strength.

Sura 5/48 of the Qur'an teaches: "If God had so willed, He would have made all of you one community, but [He has not done so so] that He may test you in what He has given you; so, compete with one another in good works. To God, you shall return, and He will tell you [the truth] about that which you have been disputing."

Chapter 8

Reflections on Jewish and Christian Encounters with Buddhism

"A thousand years hence, historians will look back at the twentieth century and remember it not for the struggle between Liberalism and Communism but for the momentous human discovery of the encounter between Christianity and Buddhism."–Arnold Toynbee. Since the 1960s, many Americans have immersed themselves in the study and practice of Buddhism. It is estimated that of the three million Buddhists in America, one million are converts from Christianity and Judaism. Many arguably engage in cross-cultural encounters with Buddhism, leading some Christian and Jewish leaders to oppose this trend as a threat to their own religions. Other leaders see nothing to fear in such encounters with Buddhism, claiming it leads to a deeper commitment to their own traditions and the betterment of humanity.

Because of the complexity and diversity within Judaism, Christianity, and Buddhism, I will focus on the responses of leading Jewish and Roman Catholic Christians to Theravada Buddhism and to the Zen School in Mahayana, the two forms of Buddhism to which many Americans are drawn and with which I have some personal experience.

The Jewish-Buddhist Encounter

Historically, Judaism has largely been interpreted by its thinkers as the only true religion. This does not mean, however, that members of other faiths may not attain salvation. According to the Talmudic Doctrine of the Seven Commandments of the Sons of Noah, "the righteous of all nations have a share in the world to come;" that is, all human beings can attain salvation who establish courts of law and who refrain from idolatry, murder, blasphemy against God, incest, theft, and eating the limb of a live animal. The consensus among traditional Jewish commentators is that Christianity and Islam worship are not idolatrous, although some question the monotheistic nature of Christianity because of the doctrine of the Trinity and the Incarnation. The worship of Asian religions, on the other hand, is viewed as *avodah zarah* (literally, strange worship) and is therefore in violation of the Noahide Law against idol worship.

With some exceptions, Orthodox rabbis generally agree with Rabbi Avigdor Miller (1908–2001) that "Buddhism, Shintoism, and all other religions of the Far East are forms of idol worship."[179] For Rabbi Miller, the Torah contains all the knowledge that is necessary for Jews, and even to study another religious tradition is an affront to God.

This attitude toward the study of alien texts is evident in Rabbi Chaim Zvi Hollander's reaction to Rabbi Zalman Schachter's suggestion that it is permissible to explore Asian forms of spirituality. Hollander charges that "Zalman Schachter's incredible advice is a direct contradiction of the Almighty's request that we not seek out and explore the spiritual modes of the *Goyim*, even if it is for the purpose of enhancing our spiritual experience in the service of our

God."[180] He further states that "the practice of any religion other than Judaism is for a Jew an act of *avodah zara*."[181]

For Rabbis Miller and Hollander, blending Judaism with the Buddhist tradition, which is not concerned with a creator God, and which rejects the idea of self, is inconceivable and particularly dangerous. Irving Greenberg, one of the outstanding liberal Orthodox rabbis of our generation, disagrees. After meeting with the Dalai Lama, he wrote, "the Dalai Lama taught us a lot about Buddhism, even more about *menschlichkeit*, and most of all about Judaism."[182] Rabbi Greenberg may not encourage Buddhist meditation, but he is certainly not opposed to the study of Buddhism and dialogue with Buddhists. More recently, he stated: "Any claim that one understanding of God is the definitive, superior one is a form of idolatry."[183] He goes on to say, "God, too, has many messengers. Pluralism leads me to recognize that the overflowing love of the Divine is never exhausted. My presence, my mind, my revelation, no matter how great, cannot exhaust infinity."[184]

Perhaps most surprising is the view of Adin Steinsaltz, the renowned rabbi and scholar who successfully undertook the monumental task of translating the entire Talmud. To my knowledge, he is the first Orthodox rabbi who makes a case for including Buddhism in the Noahide laws:

> One of the highest principles of the Noahide laws is belief in one God... By the standards of Jewish law as applied to Jews, Hinduism and Buddhism do not count as monotheistic traditions. However, the essential point of the Noahide laws is that the standards of Jewish law do not apply to non-Jews. Radically pure monotheism is expected by Judaism only from Jews. The Noahide laws do not

preclude gentile religions from developing softer, more complex, and compromised forms of monotheism. Under the Noahide laws, it is possible to assume that Hinduism and Buddhism are sufficiently monotheistic in principle for moral Hindus and Buddhists to enter the gentiles' gate into heaven.[185]

Alan Lew, a Conservative rabbi who spent ten years at a Zen Buddhist monastery practicing meditation, maintains that some forms of Buddhist meditation are not necessarily in conflict with Judaism and can actually enrich Jewish spiritual life.[186] Shelia Weinberg, a Reform rabbi who has taught Buddhist meditation to many rabbis, states: "The impact of Buddhism on my life as a Jew has been to give me a new lens with which to interpret and understand the sacred teachings of my people and more deeply apply those teachings to my life. To what end? To live with more awareness, more compassion, more wisdom, and more love."[187]

Jerome (Yehuda) Gellman, an Orthodox Jewish philosopher, presents an insightful and innovative view of Theravada and Zen Buddhism in his essay, "Judaism and Buddhism: A Jewish Approach to a Godless Religion." He writes, "I have learned of ways of holiness that I would not have imagined as a Jew. Buddhism has deeply affected my spiritual inwardness, even though I neither worship the Buddha nor believe in the cycle of rebirth."[188] Gellman acknowledges that "as Buddhism developed it became more explicitly atheistic,"[189] but points to the radical difference between Western atheism and Buddhist atheism: "Western atheism is grounded in the belief that humanity through human 'reason' replaces God and takes its destiny into its own hands."[190] On the other hand, the major concern of

Buddhists is that belief in God and a permanent self can become an attachment, which they see as an obstacle to liberation. The Buddhist motivation for atheism, therefore, is to diminish all thoughts of the self, to forget the self. Gellman finds this self-decentering, which is also found in Jewish sources, to be very valuable as a way to serve God for God's sake, rather than from egocentric motives. He writes: "Given this partial commonality, a traditional Jew such as myself can discover in Buddhism practices for self-decentering that does not exist in Judaism." He further agrees with the Buddhist view that "belief in the God of theism could easily descend into an egocentric exercise, in which God serves our needs and protects us. When that happens, devotion to God is a screen for craving our own well-being." He concludes: "Engaging in Buddhist spiritual practices for self-nullification, which for the moment leaves God out of the picture, can be an effective, welcome corrective for a traditional Jew to the dangers inherent in theistic religions, and can reinforce the worship of God from love, all by weakening an egocentric pull to God."[191]

The Christian-Buddhist Encounter

The predominant Christian attitude toward other religious faiths throughout the ages is one of exclusivism, which claims that Christianity is the only true path to salvation. In support of their position, exclusivists point to Biblical passages such as, "I am the way and the truth, and the life. No one comes to the Father except by Me (John 14:6)." Throughout its history, the Roman Catholic Church has supported a literal interpretation of the previous passage. The Fourth Lateran Council (1215), for example, ruled: "There is one universal church of believers, outside which there is no salvation at all for any."[192] Buddhism was seen as idolatrous and atheistic and inherently false. Despite *Nostra Aetate*, issued by the Second Vatican Council in 1965, which holds that "the Catholic Church rejects nothing that is true and holy in [other] religions," urges its followers to "prudently and lovingly" engage in "dialogue and collaboration with those of other religions," and to "acknowledge, preserve, and promote the spiritual and moral goods" found in these religions, the Vatican's negative attitude towards the Buddhist tradition has persisted (Vatican Council II 1966, 660; 662-663).

Pope John Paul II was deeply involved with the Second Vatican Council and one of the strong supporters of *Nostra Aetate*, yet his view of the Buddhist tradition was far from positive, as expressed in his book, "*Crossing the Threshold of Hope*:

> The "enlightenment" experience by Buddha comes down to the conviction that the world is bad, that it is a source of evil and of suffering for man.[193]

> Buddhism is in large measure an *"atheistic" system*. We do not free ourselves from evil through the good which comes from God; we liberate ourselves only through detachment from the world, which is bad. The fullness of such a detachment is not union with God but what is called nirvana, a state of perfect indifference with regard to the world. *To save oneself* means, above all, to free oneself from evil by becoming *indifferent to the world, which is the source of evil*. This is the culmination of the spiritual process.[194]

Pope John Paul II was nevertheless deeply committed to interreligious dialogue with Buddhists. Speaking to a group of Buddhists in 1980, he said, "the Catholic Church expresses her esteem for your religions and for your high spiritual values, such as purity, detachment of heart, love for the beauty of nature, and benevolence and compassion for everything that lives."[195] But while acknowledging that there are many beautiful things in Buddhism, Pope John Paul II, the most influential Christian missionary of the twentieth century, stressed that *"the mission of evangelization is an essential part of the Church."*[196] For him, blending Christianity with Buddhism is damaging to the Christian faith, a view shared by Pope Benedict XVI, who in an interview with a French magazine when he was the Prefect of the Congregation for the Doctrine of the Faith, said: "If Buddhism is attractive, it is because it appears as a possibility of touching the infinite and obtaining happiness without any concrete religious obligations. A spiritual autoeroticism [*un autoerotisme spiritual*] of some sort. Someone had rightly predicted in the 1950s that the challenge to the Church in the twentieth century would not be Marxism, but Buddhism."[197] Clearly, Pope Benedict was concerned about the many Christian-converts to Buddhism, especially Catholics, who were disproportionately leaving the Church for Buddhism.

Three Paths of the Encounter with Buddhism

As I reflect on this new phenomenon of Jews and Christians who become enticed by Buddhism, I see that they can be placed in three different categories: converts, dual-belongers, and the enriched. My hope is that these categories, though imperfect, will be as useful in understanding relationships to Buddhism as are those created by Alan Race—exclusivism, inclusivism, and pluralism—to help us understand how Christians view other religions.

The first category, converts, includes Christians and Jews who claim that they are now Buddhist. This does not mean that they no longer have a lingering attachment to their birth tradition. In rare cases, they may even reconvert, as in the case of Professor Paul Williams, who was a Buddhist for twenty years before returning to Christianity.

The second category, dual-belongers, includes people who affirm a dual religious identity. In *Buddhist and Christian? An Exploration of Dual Belonging*, Rose Drew defines this category as "people who, through their interaction with these two traditions, have reached a point where they no longer identify themselves simply as Buddhist or simply as Christian and have come to understand themselves as belonging roughly equally to both traditions."[198] Some Christians would call the dual-belongers "blenders" and view them as syncretistic. E. Burke Rochford, Jr. has found that dual-belongers do not call themselves blenders. For them, "Buddhism and Christianity stand side by side in consciousness; that one is both a Christian *and* a Buddhist. The two traditions, unique in practice and theology, are experienced as complementary and yet not to be syncretized."[199]

Most members of the Abrahamic religions have strong exclusive tendencies and find it difficult to understand dual-belongers. They see Buddhism as atheistic or polytheistic and idolatrous. Terry C. Muck, the former co-editor of the journal *Buddhist-Christian Studies,* who has a great appreciation for Buddhism, shares that he had been taught that "Buddhists were godless evildoers and pagans and barbarians."[200]

Dual-belongers are more threatening to traditional Judaism and Christianity than are people who convert to Buddhism. Sylvia Boorstein is perhaps the best-known dualbelonger. In her book, *That's Funny, You Don't Look Buddhist: On Being A Faithful Jew and a Passionate Buddhist*, she writes: "I am a real Buddhist. I'm not an ethnic Buddhist, but I'm a real Buddhist, and I'm also a Jew."[201] Christian theologian Paul Knitter, author of *Without Buddha I Could Not Be a Christian*, explained his position in a 2012 article titled, "A *'Hypostatic Union'* of Two Practices but One Person?"

> So, I am a Buddhist Christian but also a Christian Buddhist—one person with two religious natures or "principles of operation." Buddha provides the most compelling and transforming teaching and illustration of the nondual big picture, which enables me to *be peace*; Jesus offers the most compelling and transforming incarnation of how living in the big picture calls for *making peace* within this world. To have one without the other is to have neither.[202]

Those in the third and largest category, the enriched, numbering in tens of thousands, consists of Jews and Christians for whom Buddhism deepens their own faith. Many Jews and Christians have told me that their practice of Buddhist meditation has been a way for them to develop sensitivity to God and greater insight into and attachment to their own tradition. This has been my own experience. After spending two summers doing Zen meditation at Kamakura, I reread Abraham Joshua Heschel's book, *Man Is Not Alone*, and saw things that had eluded me during my previous readings. Only after an intense period of meditation did I realize they had been in front of me all the time.

The well-known Jewish philosopher, Martin Buber (1878-1965), wrote a fascinating essay on Zen Buddhism and Hasidism in which he tells the tale of Rabbi Eizik, son of Rabbi Yekel, who travels from Krakow to Prague in search of treasure. After meeting with a Christian, Rabbi Eizik ultimately discovers that the treasure was buried in his family's home in Krakow. Thus, it is a member of a different religious tradition who helps Rabbi Eizik find the treasure in Judaism, to perceive more profoundly the depth and uniqueness of his own. Sometimes we need to go to a stranger, a member of a different religious tradition, to help us find the treasure that we already possess.

Today, there is a great hunger to gain wisdom from the East. Americans in the tens of thousands have been drawn to Asian religions, especially Buddhism. Just one person, the Dalai Lama, has contributed greatly to this interest in Buddhism. Christian monks have told the Dalai Lama, a nontheist for whom Jesus is either a truly enlightened being or a Bodhisattva, that his interpretation of the Sermon on the Mount as told in his book, *The Good Heart: A Buddhist Perspective*, has made chapters 5, 6, and 7 of the Gospel of Matthew come alive for them.

More and more people realize that no religion contains all the truth, that there is always more truth to be discovered. Many of the Jews and Christians, who turn to the East for spiritual guidance, are not abandoning their own traditions. For us, the study of Asian religions and the practice of some forms of Asian meditation do not lead to a negation of God, but to a more spiritual life, a life that strives to enhance the power of human love, the power of peace, and the power of justice.

Chapter 9

Jewish and Buddhist Responses to Violence

The responses of Judaism and Buddhism towards violence are very similar, though not identical. This may seem surprising in view of the fact that the sacred texts of the monotheistic religions, including Judaism, are seen as more prone to violence than the sacred texts of Buddhist tradition that I have experienced.

The following story illustrates a Jewish view of violence:

During the First World War, the Czar's army needed troops to fight the army of the Kaiser. In order to help meet the draft quotas of the Russian army, Jewish students at many yeshivot were forced into service and sent for basic training. The students of one particular yeshivah proved to be expert sharpshooters, surpassing all other recruits with their marksmanship on the target range. Because of their skill, they were sent to the front-line trenches. As they crouched with their rifles in the trenches gazing into the mist that hovered over the field of battle, German troops suddenly advanced toward their trenches. Their Russian captain ordered the yeshivah students to open fire, but nothing happened. After his order was ignored a second time and then a third, the Russian captain began to curse them with every anti-Semitic slur he knew and threatened severe punishment. Finally, one of the students turned to the captain and said, "We'd be happy to fire, captain. But there are people in the way. As soon as the men running toward us get out of the way, we shall fire." [203]

This tale illustrates the sanctity of human life in Jewish tradition. In the Talmud, two great sages discuss the question: What constitutes the *klal gadol ba Torah*, the great principle of the Torah. For Rabbi Akiva, one of the principal shapers of Rabbinic Judaism after the destruction of the Second Temple by the Romans in 70 C.E., the answer is: "You shall love your neighbor as yourself" (Leviticus 19:18). For Ben Azzai, a scholar known for his saintliness, the answer is: "This is the book of the generations of man. In the day that God created man, in the image of God created He him. Male and female created He them" (Genesis 5:1)[204] Human beings were created in God's image (*bzelem elohim*) and are therefore precious in God's eyes and of infinite value. To murder another human being is against the Sixth Commandment, which states, *lo tirtzakh*, "You shall not murder."

According to Rabbinic Judaism, to murder another human being is to destroy the entire world, and whoever preserves a single soul, it is as though he had preserved a complete world."[205] For the rabbis, who stress that humans are created in God's image and holy, each life is both precious and irreplaceable. Rabbi Akiva taught that God is a god of pathos and is affected by what human beings do to each other. To use violence against human beings is to use violence against God. The rabbis stated: "Whoever sheds blood diminishes God's presence in the world."[206] A human may not commit murder, even to save one's own life. The Talmud records the story of the man who came before the great fourth-century rabbinic sage, Raba, and asked for guidance: "The governor of my town has ordered me 'Go and kill so-and-so, and if not, I will kill you...'" Raba replied, "Let him kill you rather than that you should commit murder. What reason do you have for thinking that your blood is redder? Perhaps his blood is redder."[207]

This is the vision of Judaism to which I was introduced as a young boy when I began my studies at Yeshiva Israel Salanter on Webster Avenue in the Bronx. Israel Salanter (1810–1883), one of the most influential Orthodox Jewish thinkers of the nineteenth century, founded the Musar Movement, an ethical movement in Judaism that is known for its stress on self-perfection.

In stressing that the primary goal of human beings is to strive for spiritual perfection, the Musar Movement has some strong affinities to the Buddhist tradition.[208] The aim of Musar is to make a human being truly human, to be a *mensch*. For a *mensch*, whose aim is to bring joy to every person one encounters, the use of violence is inconceivable. Affirming the stress on nonviolence and peace in the Jewish tradition, Isaac Bashevis Singer, in his 1978 Nobel Prize Lecture, said that the Yiddish language is "a language that possesses no words for weapons, ammunition, military exercises, war tactics..."[209]

The rabbis stated, "Great is peace, for all blessings, are contained in it... Great is peace for God's name is peace..."[210] "Great is peace because if the Jews were to practice idolatry and peace prevailed among them, God would say 'I can't punish them because peace prevails among them.'"[211] I find this third reason truly astonishing when one considers their fierce rejection of idolatry.

Though Judaism affirms that "the whole of the Torah is for the purpose of promoting peace,"[212] our tradition does not teach absolute pacifism. Teachers of the Musar Movement, for example, encouraged their students to meditate on Ecclesiastes, one of the most problematic books of the Bible. One of its familiar refrains begins with the words: "'Vanity of vanities,' said the preacher. 'Vanity of vanities. All is vanity.'" One of the reasons why everything is vanity is because of its impermanence. Musar places great stress on impermanence and, like Buddhism, encourages people to go and meditate in the graveyard. But we also find in Ecclesiastes the following statement: "A season is set for everything: a time for every experience under heaven. A time for being born and a time for dying. A time for silence and a time for speaking. A time for war and a time for peace." The rabbis who shaped the Jewish tradition looked and prayed for the coming of the Messiah who would bring complete peace:

> They shall beat their swords into ploughshares and their spears into pruning hooks. Nation shall not lift up sword against nation, neither shall they experience war anymore. (Isaiah 2:4)

But until the Messiah comes, human beings have a right to self-defense. A well-known rabbinic statement on this issue states: "If a man comes to slay you, forestall by slaying him."[213] You certainly may not kill the person who comes to kill you if you can somehow stop him without killing him, but if that is not possible, you may, as a last resort, kill him to protect your life. However, if you know that by using violence, both of you will die, then you permit yourself to be killed without killing your enemy. So, violence may become a tragic necessity. But when it does, it is always seen as a time of grief, not joy. The rabbis opposed absolute pacifism because not opposing evil and violence could contribute to injustice and violence.

The Buddhist tradition, with its stress on compassion, mercy, and peace, condemns all violence. Yet, in practice, the Buddhist response to violence seems to have has a strong affinity to the Jewish response in practice, if not always in theory. Although there are some Buddhists, such as Thich Nhat Hanh, who teach total nonviolence, most of the Buddhist writings that I have read seem to be open to the possibility that there are circumstances where violence is permitted. In an article titled, "War or Peace?" Jose Cabezon points out that "in some Mahayana texts, there are rare justifications for violence to protect the lives of others, but the person acting must be motivated by pure compassion and be very advanced on the path so that in a sense we are no longer dealing with an ordinary act of violence."[214]

Speaking on the subject of war and peace, Professor Robert Thurman explains that the Buddhist perspective on nonviolence is complicated. He tells us how the Buddha when he was a bodhisattva, had to kill a person to save 500 people. Thurman claims, "If you stand by while one guy kills hundreds, and you can stop him, and you are not hating the person who is doing it, but on the other hand, you feel those 500 lives are valuable, and if you don't take that kind of action, sitting there all lily-white, from the Buddhist perspective, you're actually an accomplice. Of course, you should try to stop the guy without killing him. But, say, the only way you could stop him was killing him... Then you are supposed to."[215]

In Paul Williams's book, Mahayana Buddhism: The Doctrinal Foundations, I found scriptural support for Thurman's and Cabezon's position. "In the Mahaparinirvana Sutra, the Buddha describes how in a previous life he killed several Brahmins to prevent them from slandering Buddhism and to save them from the punishment they might otherwise have incurred through continuing their slander."[216] Williams also points out: "According to the Mahaparinirvana Sutra, lay followers should take up arms to defend the monastic community."[217] When the Dalai Lama, recipient of the 1989 Nobel Peace Prize and a strong promoter of pacifism, was asked if he would have also refused to take up arms against Hitler, he responded, "I don't know." He speculated that if he were in Auschwitz and had a weapon, he might have killed a few SS men in order to save a large group of people.[218] In a conversation with Robert Thurman, the Dalai Lama stated, "Under particular circumstances, the violent method—any method—can be justified."[219]

It seems to me that Buddhists may kill to defend themselves or to save lives, but, as José Cabezón makes clear, it can be done only from a heart of compassion. The Jewish sources do not place as much stress on motivation but regard the taking of life to take a life as always, a time of sadness and should not be done with hate in one's heart.

In an essay, "The Meaning of This War," my teacher, Rabbi Abraham Heschel, called war "a supreme atrocity"[220] and stated, "tanks and planes cannot redeem humanity."[221] Yet, he defended the war against Nazism as an act of self-defense. He asked us to meditate on these words of the Baal Shem Tov, the founder of Hasidism: "If a man has beheld evil, he may know that it was shown to him in order that he learn his own guilt and repent; for what is shown to him is also within him."[222] The Buddhist responses to violence I heard after 9/11 all seem to stress this point made by the Baal Shem Tov.

Heschel felt that humanity had fallen into a pit: "The mark of Cain in the face of man has come to overshadow the likeness of God."²²³ Yet Heschel never gave up hope in the prophetic dream, "a dream of a world, rid of evil by the efforts of man, by his will to serve what goes beyond his own interests."²²⁴

There are great distinctions between the teachings of Moses and of the Buddha; however, about the use of violence, they are remarkably similar.

Chapter 10

The Lotus Sutra: A Buddhist Path to Mending the World

Winston King, the noted pioneer of Buddhist studies in America, has argued that the Buddhist tradition is deeply preoccupied with personal salvation but is not at all concerned with transforming society. Writing on Theravada Buddhism, Professor King states that "one of the features of the study of Buddhism most frustrating to the Western mind is the effort necessary to discover a social philosophy within it... To tell the truth, the Buddha had little, either of concern for society as such or of firm conviction of its possible improvability."[225] According to King, this lack of interest in improving society is explained by the fact that by the time of the Buddha, there was a great deal of dissatisfaction with the world and a complete turning away from the world and all its pain.

Robert Charles Zaehner (1913-1974), the late Spalding Professor of Eastern Religions and Ethics at Oxford University, claimed that Hindus, Jains, and Buddhists held an extremely pessimistic view of this world: "And so the main preoccupation of all three religions was to become the search for a way of escape from this samsaric world into something that is beyond the passage of time the Nirvana of the Buddhists, the Brahman-Atman of the Hindus."[226] Zaehner is very critical of any form of mysticism that negates the world, which is precisely how he views the Hindu and Buddhist mystics:

> "Classical" Hinduism and Buddhism are both essentially religions of escape, and there is no doubt that they make a powerful appeal to a certain type of mind, to all, indeed, who have lost their sense of purpose, for they consider that "ordinary life is hopelessly unsatisfactory, exposed to constant pain and grief, and in any case quite futile." Such religions, though a useful antidote to the prevalent materialism, would seem to be ultimately unsatisfactory psychologically because they deprive human existence as we know it of all meaning.[227]

This vision of the Buddhist tradition supports the position of Max Weber, the eminent sociologist of religion, who claimed that for Buddhism, "salvation is an absolutely personal performance of the self-reliant individual. No one, and particularly no social community, can help him. The specific asocial character of genuine mysticism is here carried to its maximum."[228] Zaehner's and Weber's evaluation of Buddhist tradition is shared by Pope John Paul II.

Pope John Paul II on the Buddhist Tradition

The following quotations from the Holy Father's best-selling book *Crossing the Threshold of Hope* capture the pope's main assumptions about Buddhism:

> "The "enlightenment" experienced by Buddha comes down to the conviction that the world is

bad, that it is the source of evil and of suffering for man."[229]

Buddhism is in large measure an *"atheistic" system*. We do not free ourselves from evil through the good which comes from God; we liberate ourselves only through detachment from the world, which is bad. The fullness of such a detachment is not union with God but what is called nirvana, a state of perfect indifference with regard to the world. *To save oneself* means, above all, to free oneself from evil by becoming *indifferent to the world, which is the source of evil*. This is the culmination of the spiritual process.[230]

Buddhists throughout the world were deeply offended by the pope's negative description of their tradition. When John Paul went to Sri Lanka in January 1995, the Catholic bishops made a public apology, insisting that the pope had not meant to hurt the feelings of Buddhists.[231]

Many Buddhists would not be upset by someone describing their tradition as atheistic or not being preoccupied with the idea of a supreme being. On the contrary, they would argue that Buddha did not believe in a theistic concept of God, that we must free ourselves from an attachment to the false idea of God, which they believe has caused serious problems for humanity.

Most problematic for Buddhists is the pope's claims that "according to Buddhism the world is bad, that it is the source of evil and suffering for man" and that nirvana is "a state of perfect indifference with regard to the world." They would argue that the world is not bad; the source of our suffering is our own desires, our thirst, greed, and clinging to the illusion of a permanent self. Only when we free ourselves from the false notion of a permanent self can earth become for us a paradise.

Western critics who call Buddhism pessimistic misread the first of the four Noble Truths. It does teach that life is suffering but then goes on to tell us that we can overcome suffering by extinguishing the greed from which it derives. Nirvana is not, as the pope claims, "a state of perfect indifference with regard to the world." Rather, it is seeing the world with newly awakened eyes. Through the process of meditation, we can totally transform the way we see the world. After attaining nirvana, the Buddha did not leave the world but devoted the next forty-five years of his life to teaching humanity that joy in this life can be attained by being more present in the world.

Western critics of Buddhism err when they claim that Buddhism is preoccupied with personal salvation to the exclusion of social transformation. My understanding that the aim of Buddhism is not only to perfect character but also to beautify the entire universe aligns with that of the British scholar of Buddhism, Trevor Ling:

To speak of Buddhism as something concerned with the private salvation of the individual soul is to ignore entirely the basic Buddhist repudiation of the notion of the individual soul. The teaching of the Buddha was not concerned with the private destiny of the individual, but with something much wider, the whole realm of a sentient being, the whole of consciousness. This inevitably entailed a concern with social and political matters, and these receive a large share of attention in the teaching of the Buddha as it is represented in the Pali texts.[232]

A moving statement by a young Western Buddhist priest, written shortly before she died, speaks directly to this controversial issue:

> I'd be embarrassed to tell anyone, it sounds so wishy-washy, but now I have maybe 50 or 60 years (who knows?) of time of a life, open, blank, ready to offer. I want to live it for other people. What else is there to do with it? Not that I expect to change the world or even a blade of grass, but it's as if to give myself is all I can do, as the flowers have no choice but to blossom... So, I must go deeper and deeper and work hard, no longer for me but for everyone I can help... Thus, I should also work politically, work to make people's surroundings that much more tolerable, work for a society that fosters more spiritual, more human values. A society for people, not profits.[233]

The Lotus Sutra: A Path to Individual and Social Healing and Transformation

The Lotus Sutra is the most influential sutra for East Asian Buddhists. Scholars of Buddhism speak of it as the Bible of Mahayana Buddhism. The Lotus itself claims that it is the most excellent teaching that leads to supreme, perfect enlightenment.

The question arises: Is the Lotus Sutra concerned only with personal transformation, or does it also call for a remake of society? My contention is that the Lotus Sutra is both a call for personal and social change and can therefore serve as a rich source for those who aspire to transform society in the twenty-first century.

Many of the key concepts of the Lotus are found in the moving parables throughout the text. Two of the central concepts developed in the sutra are the idea of one vehicle and the doctrine of skillful means. In the second chapter of the sutra, the Buddha explains to Sariputra, one of his principal disciples, that there is only one vehicle, not three, through which all human beings become buddhas. He explains that the vehicles of the *sravaka* and *pratyekabuddha* do not lead to perfect enlightenment. These two paths are presented only as a device to encourage people to enter the one true path, the path of the bodhisattva. The device is needed because most people are not sufficiently mature to receive the final message found in the Lotus Sutra.

These two central concepts are illustrated in the first parable in the Lotus Sutra, the parable of the burning house. It is retold by Leon Hurvitz in the introduction to his translation of the Lotus Sutra:

> A rich man had a very large house. The house had only one entrance, and the timber of which it was made had dried out thoroughly over the years. One day the house caught fire, and the rich man's many children, heedless of the fire, continued to play in the house. Their father called to them from outside that the house was afire and that they would perish in the flames if they did not come out. The children, not knowing the meaning of "fire" and "perish," continued to play as before. The man called out once more, "Come out, children, and I will give you ox-drawn carriages, goat-drawn carriages, and deer-drawn carriages!" Tempted by the desire for new playthings, the children left the burning house, only to find a single great ox-drawn carriage awaiting them[234]

Just as the father devised a scheme of three different carts in order to save the children, but only gave them one cart, the Buddha, using skillful means, speaks of three paths to salvation, when in fact there is only one true path, the path of the bodhisattva.

The critical point to consider is what distinguishes the *sravaka* and *pratyekabuddha* from the bodhisattva. In order to answer this question, I will briefly consider how the bodhisattva is characterized in Mahayana Buddhism. The major characteristic of bodhisattvas is their great love and compassion for all human beings. Robert Thurman calls bodhisattvas "Buddhist messiahs."[235]

Although there are major differences between the concepts of the messiah and the bodhisattva, there are also essential affinities. According to the Jewish tradition, the messiah comes to destroy evil and to bring peace, justice, and righteousness to the entire planet. The classical Jewish view of the messiah is "the prophetic hope for the end of this age, in which a strong redeemer, by his power and his spirit, will bring complete redemption, political and spiritual, to the people Israel, and along with this, earthly bliss and moral perfection to the entire human race."[236] Earthly bliss and moral perfection are precisely what the bodhisattvas aim to bring about.

The Lotus Sutra teaches that all human beings possess the buddha-nature. The bodhisattvas, therefore, make a vow to save all human beings. They do not separate their own enlightenment from that of other beings. That is the meaning of compassion (*karuna*). For the bodhisattvas, there is no wisdom (*prajna*) without compassion. A bodhisattva will not rest until all people are saved. And because all people have the buddha-nature, they will all eventually attain liberation.

From the perspective of the Lotus Sutra, paths that are monastic and escapist do not lead to perfect enlightenment because they do not show sufficient concern for society. The Lotus Sutra speaks of the arhats and *pratyekabuddhas* as "extremely conceited" because they erroneously think that they have already attained nirvana. They are, in the words of Lotus, "obsessed by utmost arrogance."[237] Full enlightenment would not only free them from conceit and arrogance but would also involve them in devoting all their energies to mending the world, which is the key characteristic of a truly enlightened being, a bodhisattva.

Unlike the classical Jewish prophet, who, according to Rabbi Abraham Joshua Heschel, is considered "a madman by his contemporaries" because of his intense indignation against injustice in society,[238] the way of the bodhisattva is different, but he is equally committed to bringing about social justice. The way of the bodhisattva reminds me of a statement by the great Hassidic teacher Rabbi Bunam, who taught: "In the psalm, we read, 'There is no peace in my bones because of my sin.' When a man has made peace within himself, he will be able to make peace in the whole world."[239]

It is clear that bodhisattvas, who postpone their own enlightenment, want to bring healing to both the individual and society, but they do this by using skillful means to heal every individual whom they encounter.

All religious traditions have an important role in mending the world, each in its own way. We need the prophets of the West and the "magnificent messiahs" of the East. Bodhisattvas and buddhas of the Lotus Sutra who make the vow to save all sentient beings and who teach that all human beings should be treated as if they were our mother can all serve as beautiful models for people who strive for personal transformation and the healing of the entire world community.

The Declaration on a Global Ethic, which was signed in September 1993 by leading religious teachers of the world who met at the Parliament of the World's Religions in Chicago, resolved that "Earth cannot be changed for the better unless the consciousness of individuals is changed first."[240] This declaration, which was signed not only by Buddhists but also by Jews, Christians, and Muslims, is in the spirit of Buddhism. The unique ways of the bodhisattva and the prophet are both working to mend the world. To bring about redemption, we need both of these paths.

Chapter 11

A Plea for Religious Humility and Justice

"Without the church, without religious institutions, I would never have been here today."

On December 5, 1999, I was fortunate to be one of the 7,000 people to hear these words spoken by President Nelson Mandela at the Parliament of the World's Religions in Cape Town, South Africa. President Mandela expressed gratitude to the audience, many of whom were religious or spiritual leaders. He told us that while he was in jail, it was Christian, Jewish, Muslim, and Hindu leaders who gave him hope that one-day apartheid would end, and he would be free.

Because I am deeply committed to promoting interfaith dialogue as a path to peace, I believe that the same change that was brought about by religious leaders in South Africa can also become a reality in America. It will require the clergy of our country to fulfill their moral obligation to teach tolerance, respect, and peace to their congregants. There are still too many clergy who remain ambivalent about such endeavors because they believe that their traditions alone represent the full truth. Therefore, they are not interested in dialogue with members of other faiths. Still, they believe that we are all children of God and that as people of faith, we must struggle against oppression.

To me, this foundation is enough for the clergy to bring healing during these difficult days in America. Yes, we have Nelson Mandela as a model, but we can also look to the Civil Rights Movement of the nineteen fifties and sixties, when Martin Luther King, Jr., a Baptist minister from the South, "the apostle for nonviolent action," asked his dear friend Rabbi Abraham Joshua Heschel, "the apostle to the Gentiles," to march with him from Selma to Montgomery to help with the struggle against the oppression of the Black community.

I believe that during this painful time of pandemics and injustice, we should look to the deep friendship and love between a Baptist minister from the South and a Polish-born Jewish rabbi from New York to inspire us to bring about meaningful change. This is the time for us to unite and help make the dream of Dr. King and Rabbi Heschel a reality. After the senseless death of George Floyd, religious and spiritual leaders, whatever their vision of truth, must stand together to fight the disease of racism.

Heschel, who was called "Father Abraham" by the Civil Rights leaders, also spoke of the need for deep humility when speaking of God, and he stated that "we are closer to God when we are asking questions than when we think we have the answers." For Heschel, "God is everywhere, save in arrogance." I believe that if more spiritual leaders would open their hearts and minds to Heschel's call for religious humility, they could influence the members of their congregations to create a better world.

I believe that what unites members of different faiths, especially of Judaism, Christianity, and Islam, is far more important than what divides them. First and foremost, they agree that all humans are created in God's image. Therefore, we must not only respect all people; we must also stand up against any form of injustice. We must never compromise with evil.

The 1974 Lausanne Covenant, which is one of the most influential documents in Evangelical Christianity, stresses social action and states that we must "denounce evil and injustice wherever they exist...[F]aith without works is dead." I believe that this, and similar statements by other denominations, can form a foundation for the clergy of all traditions to unite and make a substantial contribution in the right for racial justice.

In 1963, Rabbi Heschel sent a telegram to President John F. Kennedy in which he stated that as long as we continued to humiliate the Black community, "we forfeit the right to worship God." That same year, in a speech Heschel gave at the National Conference on Religion and Race, where Rabbi Heschel first met Martin Luther King Jr., he spoke of how his heart breaks because of our indifference to evil and of the "monstrosity of inequality." He further stated that "prayer and prejudice can't dwell in the same heart." He asserted that "worship without compassion is...An abomination."

I began with the voice of one man, President Nelson Mandela, and then turned to speak about my teacher, Abraham Joshua Heschel, and his dear friend, Martin Luther King Jr. I could also point to a religious Muslim leader, Ako Abdul-Samad, the president of the African American Association in Iowa, the nearly seventy-year-old man who stayed up until 2:00 a.m. in order to prevent violence and to bring peace and comfort to the marchers in Des Moines.

In closing, may I suggest that in this turbulent time we all ponder these words of Rabbi Heschel: "We must believe that, morally speaking, there is no limit to the concern one must feel for the suffering of human beings, that indifference to evil is worse than evil itself, that in a free society some are guilty, but all are responsible.

Appendix I

Photographs

Harold with his parents, sisters, and family friends, circa 1945

Harold's Grandmother, Mina Katzerginski

Earliest known photo of Harold, his sisters, and relatives, circa 1944

Harold and friend in Ulm, circa 1946

Bad Reichenhall, circa 1947

1949 at Coney Island beach

Harold as Samuel Sterner Choir member

Present-day photo of Kasimow home in Dryswiaty 1941

Harold Kasimow 1961 US Army

Harold with Pope John Paul II, Vatican 1998

Harold Kasimow and Alan Race with Pope Francis, Vatican 2018

Harold with Stanislaw Obirek, well-known Polish intellectual, and former Jesuit priest

Harold Kasimow and Bhai Sahib Bhai Mohinder Singh, who is one of the most influential Sikhs

Huston Smith, Harold Kasimow, and Leonard Swidler

Harold Kasimow and Master Hsin-Tao, founder of the Museum of World Religions, Cape Town

Turmantas 2001

Paneriai Memorial near Vilnius 2001

Tibetan Master Tulku Thondup and Harold Kasimow, Jerusalem

Harold Kasimow received the DA Certificate of Appreciation after the Holocaust Days of Remembrance talk at Rock Island Arsenal, May 7, 2019

Holocaust Days of Remembrance talk at Rock Island Arsenal, May 7, 2019

Notes

[1] Solomon Schechter (1847–1915) in his classic book Aspects of Rabbinic Theology: Major Concepts of the Talmud (New York: Schocken Books, 1961; originally published 1909) presents a helpful analysis of holiness in rabbinic literature. He discerns a distinction between holiness and saintliness which is not always made clear by the rabbis. In his discussion of holiness and saintliness, he states that "the former moves more within the limits of the Law, though occasionally exceeding it, while the latter, aspiring to a superior kind of holiness, not only supplements the Law, but also proves a certain corrective to it" (201). His later comment on rabbinic Judaism is very helpful in showing the affinity between Judaism and Christianity: "Impure thinking was, in the Rabbinic view, the antecedent to impure doing, and the ideal saint was as pure of heart as of hand, acting no impurity and thinking none" (210–211).

[2] Jesus was reflecting Jewish thinking when he cited these two commandments as the most important verses of the Torah. See Mark 12:28–34.

[3] The ethical classic Pirke Avot, the best-known rabbinic text, teaches that "the ignoramus will not be saintly." Pirke Avot: A Modern Commentary on Jewish Ethics. Ed. and trans. by Leonard Kravitz and Kerry M. Olitzky (New York: UAHC Press, 1993), 21 (Avot 2:5). Pirke Avot is the only part of the Talmud that was incorporated into the Jewish prayer book. The rabbis stated: "Whoever aspires to saintliness, let him fulfill the teaching of avot" (Baba Kamma, 30a).

[4] Jewish mystics go even further. For them, the words of the Torah are a rendezvous point where humans meet God, who is "in the letters of the Torah." So, study is a way toward devekut, and not only a way of discerning God's will.

[5] In his chapter "The Gaon, Rabbi Elijah Wilna," written in 1928, Louis Ginzberg writes: "The earliest documents in which the Gaon is mentioned, one dating from the time he was thirty, the other from a time when he was thirty-five, call him Rabbi Elijah the Saint, and to this day his synagogue in

Wilna is known as the synagogue of the saint..." Students, Scholars and Saints (New York: Meridian Books, 1960; originally published 1928), 141.

[6] Louis Jacobs, "The Doctrine of the Zaddik in the Thought of Elimelech of Lizensk," The Rabbi Louis Feinberg Memorial Lecture in Judaic Studies, University of Cincinnati, February 9, 1978, (page 3 in pamphlet of text). Jacobs claims that according to Elimelech of Lizensk "the Zaddik has power over life and death." This power is given by God to the tzaddik because "God so desires the prayers of the righteous" (page 6). To this day, many Hasidim visit the graves of their Hasidic masters because they believe that their masters still retain their miracle-making powers and may intervene on their behalf. In a recent pioneering work entitled Workers of Wonders, Byron Sherwin argues that the most influential Jewish leaders throughout history were also miracle workers. The veneration of saints who are believed to be miracle workers was an especially widely practiced phenomenon among North African Jews, who continue this practice today in Israel. (See Alex Weingrod, The Saint of Beersheba (Albany: State University of New York Press, 1990), and Byron L. Sherwin, Workers of Wonders: A Model for Effective Religious Leadership from Scripture to Today (Lanham, MD: Rowman and Littlefield, 2004). For a more in-depth discussion of the idea of drawing down divine grace, see Byron L. Sherwin, Kabbalah: An Introduction to Jewish Mysticism (New York: Rowman and Littlefield, 2006), especially chapter 7. I am deeply grateful to Byron Sherwin for his careful reading of this essay and for his helpful comments.

[7] Jonathan Sacks, To Heal a Fractured World: The Ethics of Responsibility (New York: Schocken Books, 2005), 245. Emphasis in the original.

[8] Immanuel Etkes, Rabbi Israel Salanter and the Mussar Movement: Seeking the Torah of Truth (Philadelphia: The Jewish Publication Society, 1993), 18.

[9] Abraham Joshua Heschel, A Passion for Truth (New York: Farrar, Straus and Giroux, 1973), 82.

[10] Heschel, A Passion, 82.

[11] Steven D. Fraade, "Ascetical Aspects of Ancient Judaism" in Arthur Green, ed., Jewish Spirituality: From the Bible through the Middle Ages (New York: Crossroad Publishing Co., 1986), 274–75.

[12] Heschel, A Passion, 25.

[13] Heschel, A Passion, 24.

[14] Quoted in Allan Nadler, The Faith of the Mithnagdim: Rabbinic Responses to Hasidic Rapture (Baltimore: Johns Hopkins University Press, 1997), 86.

[15] Moses Hayyim Luzzatto, Mesillat Yesharim ("The Path of the Upright"). Translated by Mordecai M. Kaplan (Philadelphia: The Jewish Publication Society of America, 1966), 442. I find it somewhat paradoxical that Kaplan (1881–1983), the founder of the Reconstructionist Movement in Judaism, whose reinterpretation of the Jewish tradition rejects the concept of a supernatural God, devoted so much time to translating a text written by one of the greatest mystics that Judaism has produced. In the introduction Kaplan explains why he did so: "Mesillat Yesharim will ever serve as a true mirror reflecting the inwardness and spirituality which Judaism demanded of those who lived in conformity with its laws" (xxxvi).

[16] Quoted in Luzzatto, 18.

[17] Luzzatto, 32.

[18] Luzzatto, 36.

[19] Luzzatto, 56.

[20] Luzzatto, 80.

[21] Luzzatto, 98.

[22] Luzzatto, 134.

[23] Luzzatto, 234.

[24] Luzzatto, 262. The English translation of Mesillat Yesharim by Shiraga Silverstein translates this Hebrew passage as "first sin" rather than "original sin," which I believe is more in accord with Luzzatto's meaning and the Jewish tradition, which rejects the idea of original sin (New York and Jerusalem: Feldheim Publishers, 1966), 197.

[25] Luzzatto, 266. With the focus on abstinence Luzzatto comes dangerously close to creating a monastic movement within Judaism. Following this idea to its logical conclusion one should not marry. Any man who reached this stage would be faced with a real conflict, since he must fulfill the commandment to "be fruitful and multiply." Luzzatto himself was married and had children, for he could not go against the Torah.

It may be asked whether Luzzatto's emphasis on otherworldliness is consistent with what may be called normative Judaism. Dr. Guttmann's statement concerning the very influential medieval Jewish ethical writer Bahya ibn Pakuda helps us understand this point: "Bahya goes far beyond the clues provided by the Talmud; for though the Talmud places man's ultimate aim in the world to come, it does not view the moral and religious task of his life exclusively from the viewpoint of the hereafter" (Julius Guttmann, Philosophies of Judaism: The History of Jewish Philosophy from Biblical Times to Franz Rosenzweig [New York: Anchor Books, 1966], 123). Seeing the world from the point of view of the world to come is precisely what Luzzatto does throughout his book.

[26] Luzzatto, 276.

[27] Luzzatto, 284.

[28] Luzzatto, 290.

[29] Eliezer Diamond, Holy Men and Hunger Artists: Fasting and Asceticism in Rabbinic Culture (New York: Oxford University Press, 2004), 117.

[30] Luzzatto, 444 46.

[31] Luzzatto, 452.

[32] Dov Katz, The Musar Movement, tr. Leonard Oschry (Tel-Aviv: "Orly" Press, 1977), vol. 1, part 2, 138.

[33] Ibid., 120.

[34] Quoted by Dov Katz in ibid, 65. It is beyond the scope of the present essay to compare and contrast the holy person in Judaism and Buddhism. However, I want to point out that a study of the methods of training advocated by the Buddha and Israel Salanter reveals striking similarities. For example, both advocate meditation on death. I also find it quite remarkable that Salanter, like the Buddha, believes in the possibility of a radical transformation of the human being. Salanter's closest disciple, Rabbi Simcha Zissel Ziv of Kelm, Lithuania, taught "Take time, be exact, unclutter the mind." He also said, "The worst thing that can happen to a person is to remain asleep and untamed." I see these statements as central teachings of the Buddha.

[35] Mesillat Yesharim 4.

[36] Rabbi Norman Lamm, the former president of Yeshiva University in New York City, reminds us of the great popularity of Mesillat Yesharim. He writes: "Its wide popularity can be gauged by the fact that it was reprinted no less than sixty-six times in a period of one hundred and fifty-five years." Torah; Lishmah: Torah for Torah's Sake in the Works of Rabbi Hayim of Volozhin and His Contemporaries (Hoboken, NJ: Ktav Publishing House, 1989), 338.

[37] The Musar movement had its greatest strength in Lithuania, where ninety-five percent of the Jews were killed during the Holocaust. Fortunately, a few students from the yeshiva in Slabodka, which was known as "the mother of yeshivas," and from the yeshiva of Volzhin, managed to survive. In Climbing Jacob's Ladder: One Man's Rediscovery of a Jewish Spiritual Tradition, Alan Morinis, a secular Jew and a Rhodes scholar who was a professor of Asian religions, tells the incredible story of his meeting with Rabbi Yechiel Yitzchok Perr, a great contemporary Musar teacher and how his life was transformed by this encounter. (New York: Broadway Books, 2002).

[38] Samuel H. Dresner, "Abraham Joshua Heschel: The Man" in Joshua Stampfer, ed., Prayer and Politics: The Twin Poles of Abraham Joshua Heschel (Portland, OR: Institute for Judaic Studies, 1985), 30.

[39] Byron L. Sherwin, Abraham Joshua Heschel (Atlanta: John Knox Press, 1979), 1.

[40] For example, Reinhold Niebuhr spoke of Heschel as "the most authentic prophet of religious life in our culture." Quoted by Byron L. Sherwin, "Abraham Joshua Heschel," The Torch (Spring 1969): 7. Heschel's friend Martin Luther King, Jr. often spoke of Heschel as a prophet. And at a recent conference in Switzerland, Professor Stanislaw Obirek from Warsaw, Poland, the land of Heschel's birth, called

Heschel, "a real prophet." Heschel did not accept being praised as a prophet. He said that he hoped and prayed that he was "worthy of being a descendent of the prophets." See "Carl Stern's Interview with Dr. Heschel," in Moral Grandeur and Spiritual Audacity: Essays: Abraham Joshua Heschel, ed. Susannah Heschel (New York: Farrar Straus Giroux, 1996), 400.

[41] Abraham Joshua Heschel, God in Search of Man: A Philosophy of Judaism (New York: Farrar, Straus and Cudahy, 1955), 26.

[42] Ibid., 31.

[43] Ibid., 283.

[44] Ibid., 312.

[45] Quoted in Bernard S. Raskas, Jewish Spirituality and Ethics (Hoboken, NJ: Ktav Publishing House, 1990), 9.

[46] Abraham Joshua Heschel, The Earth Is the Lord's (New York: Farrar, Straus and Giroux, 1978), 20–21.

[47] Abraham Joshua Heschel, in "Carl Stern's Interview with Dr. Heschel," in Moral Grandeur and Spiritual Audacity: Essays: Abraham Joshua Heschel, ed. Susannah Heschel (New York: Farrar, Straus, and Giroux, 1996), 412.

[48] John C. Merkle, The Genesis of Faith: The Depth Theology of Abraham Joshua Heschel (New York: Macmillan Publishing Co., 1985), 26.

[49] Eugene J. Fisher, "Heschel's Impact on Catholic-Jewish Relations," in No Religion is an Island: Abraham Joshua Heschel and Interreligious Dialogue, eds. Harold Kasimow and Byron L. Sherwin (Maryknoll, NY: Orbis Books, 1991), 111.

[50] Quoted in "Session VIII: Discussion" in Vatican II: An Interfaith Appraisal: International Theological Conference, University of Notre Dame: March 2-16, 1966, ed. John H. Miller (Notre Dame, IN: University of Notre Dame Press), 373.

[51] Wilfred Cantwell Smith, The Faith of Other Men (New York: The New American Library, 1965), 121.

[52] Alan Race, editor of the journal Interreligious Insight, develops these models in great detail. See his book Christians and Religious Pluralism: Patterns in the Christian Theology of Religions (Maryknoll, NY: Orbis Books, 1983).

[53] Karl Rahner, "Christianity and the Non-Christian Religions," in Christianity and Other Religions: Selected Readings, ed. John Hick and Brian Hebblethwaite (Philadelphia: Fortress Press, 1981), 56.

[54] Ibid, 61.

[55] Pope John Paul II, "To Representatives of the Shinto Religion," Rome, February 28, 1979, in Interreligious Dialogue: The Official Teaching of

the Catholic Church 1963–1995, ed. Francesco Gioia (Boston: Pauline Books, 1997), 218.

⁵⁶ Paul F. Knitter, One Earth Many Religions: Multifaith Dialogue and Global Responsibility (Maryknoll, NY: Orbis Books, 1995), 30.

⁵⁷ John Hick, "The Next Step beyond Dialogue," in The Myth of Religious Superiority: Multifaith Explorations of Religious Pluralism, ed. Paul F. Knitter (Maryknoll, NY: Orbis Books, 2005), 6.

⁵⁸ Abraham Joshua Heschel, "No Religion is an Island," in No Religion is an Island: Abraham Joshua Heschel and Interreligious Dialogue, eds. Harold Kasimow and Byron L. Sherwin (Maryknoll, NY: 1991), 14.

⁵⁹ Abraham Joshua Heschel, The Prophets (New York: Harper and Row, 1962), 226.

⁶⁰ "No Religion is an Island," 19.

⁶¹ Ibid, 18.

⁶² Abraham Joshua Heschel, in conversation with Patrick Granfield, as quoted by Granfield in his Theologians at Work (New York: Macmillan, 1967), 78.

⁶³ Abraham Joshua Heschel, in "Two Conversations with Abraham Joshua Heschel," transcript of "The Eternal Light" program, The National Broadcasting Company, March 19, 1972, Part I, 8. Heschel was interviewed by Rabbi Wolfe Kelman.

⁶⁴ Abraham Joshua Heschel, God in Search of Man: A Philosophy of Judaism (New York: Farrar, Straus, and Cudahy, 1955), 239.

⁶⁵ Ibid, 240.

⁶⁶ Ibid, 240.

⁶⁷ Ibid, 245.

⁶⁸ Abraham Joshua Heschel, "No Religion is an Island," 12.

⁶⁹ The Dalai Lama, The Bodhgaya Interviews, ed. Jose Ignacio Calbezon (Ithaca, NY: Snow Lion Publications, 1988), 23.

[70] The Dalai Lama, Ethics for the New Millennium (New York: Riverhead Books, 1999), 225–26.

[71] Abraham Joshua Heschel, The Insecurity of Freedom: Essays on Human Existence (New York: Schocken Books, 1966), 98.

[72] Ursula M. Niebuhr, "Notes on a Friendship: Abraham Joshua Heschel and Reinhold Niebuhr," in Abraham Joshua Heschel: Exploring His Life and Thought, ed. John C. Merkle, New York: Macmillan, 1985, 37.

[73] Daniel Berrigan, To Dwell in Peace: An Autobiography. San Francisco: Harper Collins, 1988, 179.

[74] Thomas Merton, Turning Toward the World: The Journals of Thomas Merton, Vol. 4 (1960-63), New York: Harper Collins, 1996, 61-62.

[75] Heschel, quoted in "Conversation with Martin Luther King," Conservative Judaism 22 (Spring 1968), 1.

[76] Martin Luther King, "Conversations with Martin Luther King," Conservative Judaism 22 (Spring 1968), 2.

[77] Abraham Joshua Heschel, "Religion and Race," in The Insecurity of Freedom: Essays on Human Existence. Philadelphia: The Jewish Publication Society of America, 1966, 87.

[78] Byron L. Sherwin, Abraham Joshua Heschel, Atlanta: John Knox Press, 1979, 6.

[79] Abraham Joshua Heschel, "The Moral Outrage of Vietnam", in Robert McAfee Brown, Abraham Joshua Heschel, and Michael Novak, Vietnam: Crisis of Conscience, New York: Herder and Herder, 1967, 49.

[80] Harold Flender, "Conversation with Dr. Abraham Joshua Heschel," Women's American Ort Reporter, January/February 1971, 3.

[81] In 1950, after a number of meetings with Friedman, Heschel wrote the following note to Louis Finkelstein, the president of Jewish Theological Seminary: "Dr. Friedman is endowed with a rare gift of mind and spirit and, if properly guided, he may make an important contribution to religious thinking."

[82] Maurice Friedman, "Abraham Heschel among Contemporary Philosophers: From Divine Pathos to Prophetic Action," Philosophy Today, Winter 1974, 303.

[83] Maurice Friedman, The Hidden Human Image: A Heartening Answer to the Dehumanizing Threats of our Age, New York: Dell, 1974, 344.

[84] Ibid, 348.

[85] Ibid, 351.

[86] Martin Luther King, Jr. "Remaining Awake During a Revolution." Address delivered at Grinnell College, Grinnell, Iowa, October 29, 1967. Heschel remains the most important spiritual guide for many of his students. He also changed the lives of people who were not officially his students, including his biographer Edward Kaplan and Arnold Eisen, the chancellor of Jewish Theological Seminary of America, who wrote that Heschel "changed my life."

[87] Abraham Joshua Heschel, "The White Man on Trial," in The Insecurity of Freedom: Essays on Human Existence, Philadelphia: The Jewish Publication Society of America, 1966, 107.

[88] Edward K. Kaplan, Spiritual Radical: Abraham Joshua Heschel in America, 1940-1972, New Haven: Yale University Press, 2007, 120.

[89] Maurice Friedman, The Human Way: A Dialogic Approach to Religion and Human Experience, Chambersburg, PA: Anima Books, 1982, 183.

[90] Abraham Joshua Heschel, Man Is Not Alone: A Philosophy of Religion, Philadelphia: The Jewish Publication Society of America, 1951, 236-37.

[91] The Papers of Martin Luther King, Jr., Vol. VI, ed. By Clayborne Carson, Berkeley: University of California Press, 2007, 472.

[92] Abraham Joshua Heschel, "Choose Life," in Moral Grandeur and Spiritual Audacity: Essays, ed. Susannah Heschel, New York: Farrar, Straus, Giroux, 1996, 255.

[93] Ibid, 255-256.

[94] Martin Luther King, Jr., The Words of Martin Luther King, Jr. ed. Coretta Scott King, New York: Newmarket Press, 1984, 85.

[95] Maurice Friedman, The Hidden Human Image: A Heartening Answer to the Dehumanizing Threats of our Age, New York: Dell, 1974, 367.

[96] Abraham Joshua Heschel, "No Religion is an Island," in No Religion is an Island: Abraham Joshua Heschel and Interreligious Dialogue, eds.

Harold Kasimow and Byron L. Sherwin, Maryknoll, New York: Orbis Books, 1991, 14.

[97] Abraham Joshua Heschel, in conversation with Patrick Granfield, as quoted by Granfield in his Theologians at Work, New York: Macmillan, 1967, 78.

[98] Maurice Friedman, Touchstones of Reality: Existential Trust and the Community of Peace, New York: E.P. Dutton. 1972, 214.

[99] See Harold Kasimow, Divine-Human Encounter: A Study of Abraham Joshua Heschel, Washington, D.C.: University Press of America, 1979, 82. The foreword to this published version of my dissertation was written by Maurice Friedman.

[100] This essay was sent to me by Maurice Friedman in 1986. To my knowledge this is the first time it has been published.

[101] Heschel, No Religion is an Island, 18-19.

[102] Heschel, No Religion is an Island, 22.

[103] The Papers of Martin Luther King, Jr., Vol. VI, ed. By Clayborne Carson, Berkeley: University of California Press, 2007, 147.

[104] Lewis V. Baldwin, To Make the Wounded Whole: The Cultural Legacy of Martin Luther King, Jr. Minneapolis: Augsburg Fortress, 1992, 145.

[105] See Friedman's A Heart of Wisdom: Religion and Human Wholeness, Albany: State University of New York Press, 1992, especially Part Two, and his Intercultural Dialogue and the Human Image New Delhi: D.K. Printworld (P) Ltd, 1995.

[106] Martin Luther King, Jr., Why We Can't Wait, New York: New American Library, 1964, 80.

[107] King, Jr., Why We Can't Wait 82. In a note in his book Martin Buber's Life and Work: The Later Years, 1945-1965, Friedman claims, after writing to Coretta King, that when King went to prison, he took two books with him: Camus's The Rebel and Between Man and Man by Martin Buber. 450.

[108] His love and reverence for the Hebrew Bible brings Friedman together with Heschel and King. Also, Friedman, like Heschel, was deeply influenced by the Hasidic tradition.

[109] Byron Sherwin, a disciple of Heschel, writing on the Holocaust, stated that Jews in Nazi Germany "were targeted essentially on racial and not on religious grounds," in "Conceptions, Misconceptions and Implications of the Holocaust: A Jewish Perspective." Shofar. Summer 1986, 9.

[110] Abraham Joshua Heschel, "The Religious Basis of Equality of Opportunity—The Segregation of God" in Race: Challenge to Religion, Mathew Ahmann, ed, Chicago: Henry Regnery Company, 1963, 56.

[111] Ibid, 63.

[112] Ibid, 67.

[113] Abraham Joshua Heschel, Who Is Man?, Stanford: Stanford University Press, 1965, 25.

[114] Heschel, "The Religious Basis of Equality of Opportunity," in Mathew Ahmann, ed., Race: Challenge to Religion (Chicago: Henry Regnery Company, 1963), 158.

[115] Heschel, "The Religious Basis of Equality of Opportunity," 66.

[116] Martin Luther King, Jr., "A Challenge to the Churches and Synagogues," in Mathew Ahmann, ed., Race: Challenge to Religion (Chicago: Henry Regnery Company, 1963), 158.

[117] King, Jr., "A Challenge to the Churches and Synagogues," 168.

[118] Susannah Heschel, "Theological Affinities in the Writings of Abraham Joshua Heschel and Martin Luther King, Jr.," Conservative Judaism Vol. 50: 2-3, Winter/Spring 1998, 127.

[119] Ibid, 129.

[120] Hans Küng, "Christianity and World Religions: Dialogue with Islam," in Toward a Universal Theology of Religion, ed. Leonard Swidler (Maryknoll, New York: Orbis Books, 1987), 194.

[121] Quoted in Swami Nikhilananda, Vivekananda: A Biography (New York: RamakrishnaVivekananda Center, 1953), 185.

[122] Abraham Joshua Heschel, God in Search of Man: A Philosophy of Judaism (New York: Farrar, Straus and Cudahy, 1955), 28–29.

[123] Ibid, 29.

[124] Quoted in Ainslie T. Embree, The Hindu Tradition (New York: Vintage Books, 1972), 322.

[125] Abraham Joshua Heschel, "The Concept of Man in Jewish Thought" in The Concept of Man, ed S. Radhakrishnan and P. T. Raju, (London: Allen and Unwin, 1960), 128.

[126] Quoted in Swami Nikhilananda, Vivekananda: A Biography (New York: RamakrishnaVivekananda Center, 1953), 198.

[127] Quoted in Ibid, 197.

[128] Abraham Joshua Heschel, Man Is Not Alone: A Philosophy of Religion (New York: Farrar, Straus and Young, 1951), 214.

[129] Abraham Joshua Heschel, "The Moral Outrage of Vietnam," in Robert McAfee Brown, Abraham J. Heschel, and Michael Novak, Vietnam: Crisis of Conscience (New York: Association Press, 1967), 50.

[130] Swami Nikhilananda, ed. Vivekananda: The Yogas and Other Works (New York: Ramakrishna-Vivekananda Center, 1953), 183.

[131] Ibid, 197.

[132] Abraham Joshua Heschel, God in Search of Man: A Philosophy of Judaism (New York: Farrar, Straus and Cudahy, 1955), 15.

[133] Abraham Joshua Heschel, "No Religion is an Island" Union Seminary Quarterly Review 21:2 (January 1966): 126. 16. Ibid.127.

[134] Ibid,127.

[135] Quoted in Christopher Isherwood, Ramakrishna and His Disciples (New York: Simon and Schuster, 1965), 264. We need not be surprised, therefore, that the Center for Integrative Education, whose "main areas of interest have been the mediation of Eastern and Western thought," realized the affinity between Heschel and Eastern thought and asked him to become a member of their Board of Correspondents. A copy of this letter, dated June 9, 1972, was given to me by Rabbi Heschel.

[136] In Religions in Dialogue: From Theocracy to Democracy. Ed. Alan Race and Ingrid Shafer. Ashgate: Burlington, VT, 2002, 30.

[137] Ibid, 34. 20. "Religious Diversity and the Millennium," Internet article at www.hartmaninstitute.com, 2001, 2. 21.

[138] "Religious Diversity and the Millennium," Internet article at www.hartmaninstitute.com, 2001, 2. 21.

[139] Jonathan Sacks, The Dignity of Difference: How to Avoid the Clash of Civilizations. London: Continuum, 2002, 64. 22.

[140] John Paul II, "Reflections on the Fiftieth Anniversary of the Uprising of the Warsaw Ghetto," in Eugene J. Fisher and Leon Klenicki, comp., ed., and commentary, The Saint for Shalom: How Pope John Paul II Transformed Catholic-Jewish Relations: The Complete Texts, 1979–2005, A Crossroad Herder Book (New York: Crossroad, 2011), 235.

[141] Quoted in James Martin, "Saint Pope John XXIII," America, April 28, 2011.

[142] Available at: http://www.vatican.va/archive/hist_councils/ii_vatican_council/documents/vat-ii_ decl _19651028_nostra-aetate_en.html.

[144] Cardinal Stanislaw Dziwisz in conversation with Gian Franco Svidercoschi, A Life with Karol: My Forty-Year Friendship with the Man Who Became Pope, tr. Adrian J. Walker (New York: Doubleday, 2008 [orig.: Una Vita con Karol (Vatican City: Libreria Editrice Vaticana, 2007)]), 160.

[144] See Jerzy Kluger, The Pope and I: How a Lifelong Friendship Between a Polish Jew and John Paul II Advanced the Cause of Jewish-Christian Relations, tr. Matthew Sherry (Maryknoll, NY: Orbis Books, 2012), 89.

[145] Abraham Joshua Heschel, "No Religion is an Island," in Harold Kasimow and Byron L. Sherwin, eds., No Religion is an Island: Abraham Joshua Heschel and Interreligious Dialogue (Maryknoll, NY: Orbis Books, 1991), 9.

[146] George Weigel, "John Paul II: A Biblical Pilgrim in the World," in David G. Dalin and Matthew Levering, eds., John Paul II and the Jewish People: A Jewish-Christian Dialogue, A Sheed & Ward Book (Lanham, MD, and Plymouth, U.K.: Rowman and Littlefield, 2008), 5.

[147] "An Historic Meeting: Pope Commits the Catholic Church to Its Ongoing Relationship and Dialogue with the Jewish Community," JTA [Jewish Telegraphic Agency], November 1, 1985; available at: http://www.jta.org/1985/11/01/archive/an-historic-meeting-pope-commits-the-catholic-church-to-its-ongoing-relationship-and-dialogue-with.

[148] Quoted in Fisher and Klenicki, Saint for Shalom, 202.

[149] Commission for Religious Relations with the Jews, Vatican Guidelines and Suggestions for Implementing the Conciliar Declaration Nostra Aetate (n. 4), December 1, 1974, preamble.

[150] Fisher and Klenicki, Saint for Shalom, 285.

[151] Ibid, 274.

[152] This was not John Paul II's first visit to a synagogue. As a youth he went to a New Year Jewish service at the synagogue in Wadowice with his Jewish friend Jerzy Kluger. On February 28, 1969, when he was already a cardinal, he visited a number of synagogues in Krakow.

[153] Quoted in Fisher and Klenicki, Saint for Shalom, 11, from National Catholic News Service, December 31, 1986.

[154] John Paul II, "To Representatives of the Jewish Community of Rome" (April 13, 1986), in Interreligious Dialogue: The Official Teaching of the Catholic Church (1963–1995), ed. Francesco Gioia (Boston, MA: Pauline Books and Media, 1997 [orig.: Il Dialogo Interreligioso (Vatican City: Libreria Editrice Vaticana, 1994)]), 530.

[155] John Paul II, "Address upon Arrival in Egypt," in Lawrence Boadt and Kevin di Camillo, eds., John Paul II in the Holy Land: In His Own Words; with Christian and Jewish Perspectives by Yehekel Landau and Michael McGarry, CSP, A Stimulus Book (New York and Mahwah, NJ: Paulist Press, 2005), 56.

[156] Quoted in Fisher and Klenicki, Saint for Shalom, 330–331.

[157] Ronald Kronish, "The Historic Visit of the Pope to Israel in March, 2000: Memories and Hopes," April 1, 2004; see http://www.jcrelations.net/The_Historic_Visit_of_the_Pope_to_Israel_in_March_2000__Memories_and_Hopes.2822.0.html?id=720&L=3&searchText=ron+Kronish&searchFilter=%2A.

[158] Ibid.

[159] Quoted in Fisher and Klenicki, Saint for Shalom, 336; emphasis in original.

[160] Quoted in Garry Wills, "The Vatican Regrets," New York Review of Books, May 25, 2000, 19; available at http://www.nybooks.com/articles/archives/2000/may/25/the-vatican-regrets/.

[161] "ADL Welcomes Pope John Paul II's Visit and Words at Yad Vashem".

[162] October 27, 2001; available at http://ccarnet.org/about-us/news-and-events/news-and-events-archive/ccar-and-rabbinical-assembly-recognize-bonds-between-jewish-and-/.

[163] George Weigel, Witness to Hope: The Biography of Pope John Paul II (New York: Cliff Street Books [Harper Collins], 1999), 848.

[164] Quoted in Byron L. Sherwin and Harold Kasimow, eds., John Paul II and Interreligious Dialogue, Faith Meets Faith Series (Maryknoll, NY: Orbis Books, 1999), 42.

[165] Seyyed Hossein Nasr, Ideals and Realities of Islam (Boston: Beacon Press, 1972), 16.

[166] Seyyed Hossein Nasr, "Response to Hans Küng's Paper on Christian-Muslim Dialogue," The Muslim World 77 (1987): 99. 9 Sayyid Abul A'la Mawdudi, Towards Understanding Islam (Gary, Ind.: International Islamic Federation of Student Organizations, 1970), 108n.

[167] Ibid, 47.

[168] Isma'il Raji al Faruqi, "Islam," in The Great Asian Religions, comp. by Wing-tsit Chan, Isma'il al Faruqi, Joseph Kitagawa, and P. T. Raju (London: Macmillan, 1969), 307.

[169] Isma'il Raji al Faruqi, Christian Ethics: A Historical and Systematic Analysis of Its Dominant Ideas (Montreal: McGill University Press, 1967), 153.

[170] Al Faruqi, "Islam," 332.

14 Isma'il Raji al Faruqi, Islam (Niles, Ill.: Argus Communications, 1979), 10–11.

15 Ibid, 5.

[171] Isma'il Raji al Faruqi, Islam (Niles, Ill.:Argus Communications, 1979), 10–11.

[172] Ibid, 5.

[173] Al Faruqi, "Islam and Christianity: Diatribe or Dialogue." Journal of Ecumenical Studies 5 (1968): 54.

[174] Seyyed Hossein Nasr, Ideals and Realities of Islam (Boston: Beacon Press, 1972), 15.

[175] Seyyed Hossein Nasr, Sufi Essays (Albany: State University of New York Press, 1972), 123.

[176] Nasr, "Response to Hans Küng's Paper," 100.

[177] "Christianity and World Religions: Discussion" The Muslim World 77 (1987): 131.

[178] Ibid, 132.

[179] Avigdor Miller, Awake My Glory (New York: Bais Yisroel of Rugby, 1980), 62.

[180] Chaim Zvi Hollander, "Beyond the Torah Limits," in Zen and Hasidism, ed. Harold Heifetz (Wheaton, Ill.: The Theosophical Publishing House, 1978), 139.

[181] Ibid, 140.

[182] Quoted in The Dalai Lama: A Policy of Kindness: An Anthology of Writings by and about the Dalai Lama, ed., Sidney Piburn (Ithaca, NY: Snow Lion Publications, 1990), 65.

[183] In Religions in Dialogue: From Theocracy to Democracy, ed. Alan Race and Ingrid Shafer (Burlington, Vt.: Ashgate, 2002), 30.

[184] Ibid, 34.

[185] Adin Steinsaltz, "Peace without Conciliation: The Irrelevance of 'Toleration' in Judaism," Common Knowledge 11:1 (2005).

[186] See Alan Lew, One God Clapping: The Spiritual Path of a Zen Rabbi (New York: Kodansha International, 1999).

[187] Sheila Peltz Weinberg, "The Impact of Buddhism" in Beside Still Waters: Jews, Christians, and the Way of the Buddha, ed. Harold

Kasimow, John P. Keenan, and Linda Klepinger Keenan (Boston: Wisdom Publications, 2003), 111.

[188] Jerome Gellman, "Judaism and Buddhism: A Jewish Approach to a Godless Religion," In Jewish Theology and World Religions, ed. Alon Goshen-Gottstein and Eugene Korn (Oxford: The Littman Library of Jewish Civilization, 2012), 301.

[189] Ibid, 305.

[190] Ibid, 309.

[191] Ibid, 314.

[192] In John H. Leith, ed., Creeds of the Churches: A Reader in Christian Doctrine from the Bible to the Present (Garden City, NY: Doubleday, 1963), 58.

[193] Pope John Paul II, Crossing the Threshold of Hope (New York: Alfred A. Knopf, 1994), 85.

[194] Ibid, 86.

[195] Pope John Paul II, in Interreligious Dialogue: The Official Teaching of the Catholic Church (1963–1995), ed. Francesco Gioia (Boston: Pauline Books, 1997), 222.

[196] Pope John Paul II, Crossing the Threshold of Hope (New York: Alfred A. Knopf, 1994), 115.

[197] Quoted in Leo D. Lefebure, "Cardinal Ratzinger's Comments on Buddhism," Buddhist-Christian Studies 18 (1998): 221.

[198] Rose Drew, Buddhist and Christian? An Exploration of Dual Belonging (Cambridge, UK: Routledge, 2011), 6.

[199] E. Burke Rochford, Jr., "Interfaith Encounter and Religious Identity: Sociological Observations and Reflections" in Beside Still Waters: Jews, Christians, and the Way of the Buddha, ed. Harold Kasimow, John P. Keenan, and Linda Klepinger Keenan (Boston: Wisdom Publications, 2003), 219.

[200] Terry C. Muck, "Living in God's Grace," in Beside Still Waters: Jews, Christians, and the Way of the Buddha, ed. Harold Kasimow, John P.

Keenan, and Linda Klepinger Keenan (Boston: Wisdom Publications, 2003), 193.

[201] Sylvia Boorstein, That's Funny, You Don't Look Buddhist: On Being a Faithful Jew and a Passionate Buddhist (New York: Harper Collins, 1997), 9.

[202] Paul F. Knitter, "A 'Hypostatic Union' of Two Practices but One Person?" Buddhist-Christian Studies 32 (2012), 26.

[203] Byron L. Sherwin, In Partnership with God: Contemporary Jewish Law and Ethics (Syracuse: Syracuse University Press,1990), 180.

[204] Jerusalem Talmud, Nedarim 9:4.

[205] Sanhedrin, 37a.

[206] Mekhilta d' Rabbi Yishmael, quoted in Sherwin, 174.

[207] Sanhedrin, 73a.

[208] The Musar Movement, like Buddhism, advocated meditation on death as a way to obliterate the ego. Israel Salantar believed that it is extremely difficult for human beings to change even a single character trait. Yet he never gave up hope in the possibility of a radical transformation of the individual: "Yet let no one say: What God has made cannot be changed. He, may He be blessed, has infused an evil drive in me; how can I ever hope to eradicate it? It is not so. Man's drives can be subdued and even changed... It is within his power to conquer his evil nature and prevent its functioning, and also to change his nature to good by study and training." (Quoted in Dov Katz, The Musar Movement, tr. Leonard Oschry, Tel-Aviv: Orly Press, 1977, vol. 1, part 2, 65.) For the most accessible book on Musar, see Alan Morinis, Climbing Jacob's Ladder: One Man's Rediscovery of a Jewish Spiritual Tradition (New York: Broadway Books, 2002).

[209] Isaac Bashevis Singer, Nobel Lecture, December 8, 1978. www.nobel.se/literature/laureates/1978/singer-lecture.html.

[210] Midrash Leviticus Rabbah 9:9.

[211] Midrash Genesis Rabbah 38:6.

[212] Talmud Gittin 59b.

[213] Sanhedrin, 72a.

[214] José Cabezón, "War or Peace?" Tricycle: The Buddhist Review, Spring 2002: 53.

[215] Quoted in William Meyers, "War and Peace and New York City: A Conversation with Robert Thurman," New York Spirit, April and May 2002.

[216] Paul Williams, Mahayana Buddhism: The Doctrinal Foundations (London: Routledge, 1989), 161.

[217] Ibid, 159.

[218] Dalai Lama, Beyond Dogma: Dialogues and Discourses, trans. Alison Anderson, ed. Marianne Dresser (Berkeley, Calif.: North Atlantic Books, 1996), 111–12.

[219] Quoted in Robert Thurman, "The Dalai Lama on China, Hatred, and Optimism," Mother Jones, November-December, 1997: 31.

[220] Abraham J. Heschel, "The Meaning of This War (World War II)," in Moral Grandeur and Spiritual Audacity: Essays by Abraham Joshua Heschel, ed. Susannah Heschel (New York: Farrar, Straus, Giroux, 1996), 211.

[221] Ibid, 209.

[222] Ibid, 212.

[223] Ibid, 209.

[224] Ibid.

[225] Winston King, In the Hope of Nibbana (LaSalle, Ill.: Open Court, 1964), 176-77.

[226] R. C. Zaehner, Hinduism (London: Oxford U. Press, 1962), 67.

[227] R. C. Zaehner, "Conclusion," The Concise Encyclopedia of Living Faiths, ed., R. C. Zaehner (Boston: Beacon Press, 1959), 415. The quote within this quote is taken from the article "Buddhism: The Mahayana" by Edward Conze printed in the same volume, 301.

[228] Max Weber, The Religion of India: The Sociology of Hinduism and Buddhism (Glencoe, Ill.: Free Press, 1958), 213.

[229] Pope John Paul II, Crossing the Threshold of Hope (New York: Knopf, 1994), 85.

[230] Ibid, 86. Italics in the original.

[231] Tad Szulc, Pope John Paul II: The Biography (New York: Scribner, 1995), 467.

[232] Trevor Ling, The Buddha: Buddhist Civilization in India and Ceylon (New York: Scribner, 1973), 122.

[233] Maura O'Halloran, Pure Heart, Enlightened Mind: The Zen Journal and Letters of Maura "Soshin" O'Halloran (Boston: Charles E. Tuttle Co., 1994), 233.

[234] "Preface," Scripture of the Lotus Blossom of the Fine Dharma, trans. Leon Hurvitz (New York: Columbia U. Press, 1976), xi.

[235] Robert A. F. Thurman, "The Buddhist Messiahs: The Magnificent Deeds of the Bodhisattvas," in The Christ and the Bodhisattva, ed. Donald S. Lopez, Jr., and Steven C. Rockefeller (Albany: State U. of New York Press, 1987), 65.

[236] Joseph Klausner, The Messianic Idea in Israel: From Its Beginning to the Completion of the Mishnah, trans. W. F. Stinespring (New York: Macmillan, 1955), 9.

[237] The Three Fold Lotus Sutra, trans. Bunno Kato, Yoshiro Tamura, and Kojiro Miyasaka (Tokyo: Kosei Publishing Co., 1975), 62.

[238] Abraham Joshua Heschel, The Prophets (New York: The Burning Bush Press, 1962), 18.

[239] Quoted in Martin Buber, Tales of the Hasidim: The Later Masters (New York: Schocken, 1948), 264.

[240] A Global Ethic: The Declaration of the Parliament of the World's Religions, ed Hans Küng and Karl-Josef Kuschel (New York: Continuum, 1993), 15.

www.ingramcontent.com/pod-product-compliance
Lightning Source LLC
Chambersburg PA
CBHW050527170426
43201CB00013B/2107